The New York Times

From the pages of *The New York Times*
Edited by Dave Anderson

This book is available in quantity at special discounts for your group or organization. For further information, contact:

Triumph Books LLC
814 N. Franklin Street
Chicago, Illinois 60610
(312) 337-0747
Fax (312) 280-5470

Printed in the United States of America
ISBN 978-1-62937-248-8

The New York Times
Project Editor: Alex Ward
Photo Editor: Phyllis Collazo

This is an unofficial publication. This book is in no way affiliated with, licensed
by, or endorsed by the Yogi Berra estate or Major League Baseball.

Front and back cover photos courtesy of AP Images.

Content packaged by Mojo Media, Inc.
Joe Funk: Editor
Jason Hinman: Creative Director

AP Images

Contents

Foreword

By Ron Guidry

Yogi Berra was my manager, my coach, my Yankees generational elder, and for an unforgettable decade and a half, my spring training companion. He became my dearest friend and was also during that period baseball's greatest ambassador, a fixture and legend, synonymous with the game.

Even if you didn't know much about baseball, you knew about Yogi Berra. His name created an instant recognition not only for older fans who could recall his long-ago career as a Hall of Fame catcher, but also for younger fans, who knew him as one of the game's great legends and characters. And for those who had the great fortune of knowing or even just meeting him, it was obvious what made him such an icon.

Some of his lasting fame no doubt was Lawrence Peter Berra's colorful nickname, given to him as a youth growing up on playing fields in his St. Louis neighborhood known as The Hill. Part of it had to do with his long association with the Yankees, baseball's most successful and identifiable franchise. But most of it had to do with the essence of the man, with what he stood for and how he represented the game. With honor, with class, and with the unshakable belief that no matter how famous he was, he was no better than anyone else.

He was a typical guy, an everyman from his modest beginnings to his average size and plainspoken ways and for how he treated people in his daily life.

It didn't matter to Yogi if you were rich and powerful like George Steinbrenner or the guy behind the counter where he bought his newspapers. If you were someone he could count on, a person who enjoyed a good chat, he would have time for you. He would listen to what you had to say about sports—and he loved all sports—and especially about baseball and the Yankees, the team he felt spiritually tied to even when he separated himself from the organization for 14 years after Steinbrenner's 1985 dismissal of him as manager through an intermediary.

As Yogi's self-exile dragged on, family members begged him to return to Yankee Stadium, but he refused. You might say he was stubborn but you also had to admit he was principled, a man of his word. That made him more of a hero for anyone who had ever been treated with disrespect in the workplace.

When the Boss finally appeared at Yogi's museum in New Jersey in January 1999 to apologize, Yogi demonstrated that he was a man of compassion and grace. He not only forgave Steinbrenner but actually became one of his most devoted defenders.

The reconciliation was great for Yogi because he was again able to go back to the clubhouse, schmooze with guys he admired, like Derek Jeter and Mariano Rivera, and go upstairs to watch a game. It was great for Steinbrenner because having Yogi Berra around your team was always a blessing. How else to explain David Cone's perfect game on July 18, 1999, during

Yogi's first season back at Yankee Stadium, on the day he was honored and with his 1956 World Series perfect game battery mate, Don Larsen, in the house?

Our spring training relationship began simply enough; he needed a ride from the airport when he came in 2000 to join those of us who worked as on-field instructors. I volunteered and immediately could tell that Yogi was a little out of sorts. He hadn't been to spring training since the team's base had moved to Tampa from Fort Lauderdale. I asked him to have supper with me that night and again the next night. Before long, it was established that he and I would be together during his spring training stays—at dinner, the golf course, shooting the breeze in the coaches' room. Yogi was a man of unbreakable routines. I was the lucky beneficiary, the chosen partner with access to his encyclopedic knowledge of baseball history.

But better yet was the opportunity to see how beloved the man really was, how badly people wanted to reach out and touch him, asking for an autograph, a handshake, or smile. It hurt Yogi to be off limits or to say no to anyone but it also got to the point where I had to lay some ground rules—otherwise we would never have gotten through dinner.

As he got older, and needed more help in getting around, I took on more responsibility in caring for Yogi, to help keep him safe. People who read about our relationship in *The New York Times* and in a subsequent book would tell me—some with tears in their eyes—how it reminded them of a relationship they'd had with an aging relative. I would tell them it was never a case of charity, or even kindness, as much as it was a privilege to spend that time when you love and respect someone as much as I did Yogi.

I think I can speak for the sport and its fans when I say that I relished every minute. ∎

Yogi Berra and Ron Guidry watch together as the All-Star Game logo is unveiled at Yankee Stadium on Tuesday, July 31, 2007. (AP Images)

Introduction

THE 8 LIVES OF NUMBER 8

By Dave Anderson

As a Yankee rookie in 1947, Lawrence Peter (Yogi) Berra was issued uniform number 35, but the next season, in the absence of coach Bill Dickey who had worn number 8 as a Hall of Fame catcher, 8 was stitched on the back of Yogi's pinstripes and road grays. For decades Yogi wore 8 as a Yankee slugger, catcher, outfielder, manager, coach, and Old-Timers Day fixture. In a 1972 ceremony, the Yankees retired his 8 (along with Dickey's 8) and no other Yankee will ever wear that number.

As if anyone could. Or would dare.

Number 8 wouldn't look right on any other Yankee except Yogi, who was sturdy and short at 5 feet, 8 inches and 191 pounds in his prime. But in retrospect now, his number 8 represents his eight lives in baseball:

1. As a teenager on the sandlots of The Hill neighborhood in St. Louis, Berra was signed by the Yankees after his hometown Cardinals ignored him. Following the 1943 season with the Norfolk (Virginia) Tars in the Class B Piedmont League, where he hit .253 with seven home runs, he enlisted in the Navy during World War II. On D-Day, he was a 19-year-old seaman first-class on a 36-foot L.C.S.S. rocket boat off Normandy. "The S.S. stood for Support Small," he recalled half a century later, "but to us the S.S. was Suicide Squad. We went in before the army. We fired our rockets, a 5-inch shell. Then the army hit the beach. When the shooting started, it looked like Fourth of July fireworks. I can still hear Ensign Holmes yelling, 'Get your head in.'" He later served off the coasts of Italy, France, and Africa before returning to the New London, Connecticut, base. "I told 'em I didn't volunteer for submarine duty," he said, remembering his New London posting with a laugh. "But they wanted me to play baseball there."

2. After Berra's discharge, playing baseball was all he did—at first for the Newark Bears in 1946 (.314, 15 homers, 59 RBIs in only 277 at-bats) then for the Yankees in a Hall of Fame career like no other in major-league history. He was: a member of 10 World Series championship teams and 14 American League pennant-winners; a three-time Most Valuable Player; holder of a .285 lifetime average with 358 homers and 1,430 RBIs; and an All-Star Game selection in 14 consecutive seasons.

3. As a rookie manager in 1964, Berra guided the Yankees through a torrid three-team pennant race with the Chicago White Sox and the Baltimore Orioles before losing the World Series to the Cardinals in seven games. Shockingly, the next day he was fired.

4. Joining the crosstown New York Mets as a coach in

1965 under Casey Stengel, his longtime Yankee manager, Berra emerged as the Mets manager in 1972 following Gil Hodges' death from a heart attack. He led the Mets to the National League pennant in 1973, but they lost the World Series to the Oakland Athletics in seven games. He was dismissed as Mets manager late in the 1975 season.

5. After rejoining the Yankees as a coach in 1976, Berra had a second term as manager in 1984 and for 16 games in 1985 before his hasty dismissal by George Steinbrenner—despite the principal owner's promise that he would last the entire season. Angered at Steinbrenner's having general manager Clyde King inform him of the decision instead of doing it personally, he vowed not to return to Yankee Stadium as long as Steinbrenner owned the franchise.

6. Beginning in 1986, he was a coach with the Houston Astros for four seasons as a favor to his longtime friend and New Jersey neighbor John McMullan, the Astros owner.

7. Still angry at Steinbrenner, he continued his self-exile from Yankee Stadium for more than 13 years, but early in 1999 he accepted Steinbrenner's personal apology at the newly opened Yogi Berra Museum and Learning Center near his Montclair, New Jersey, home and promised to return to the Stadium.

8. More than ever the homespun philosopher that his boyhood pal, Joe Garagiola, so precisely defined ("Yogi doesn't say funny things, he says things funny"), he basked in the applause on Old-Timers Day, opening day, and other Yankee occasions. This was especially true the night he wore his pinstriped uniform with 8 on the back at the ceremonies surrounding the last regular-season game in 2008 at the now demolished Yankee Stadium—where he hit so many homers, caught so many pitchers, and helped the Yankees celebrate 10 World Series titles and 14 pennants.

What a life! Or more appropriately, 8 lives for number 8. ■

Casey Stengel, then manager of the Mets, and Yogi Berra, then manager of the Yankees, talk at Shea Stadium in 1964. (Larry C. Morris/The New York Times)

Keeping the Legacy Alive

By Dave Anderson • September 24, 2015

Driving or walking, if you turn onto Yogi Berra Drive and follow it through the Montclair State campus, you'll arrive at the non-profit Yogi Berra Museum and Learning Center. Most people, upon their death, leave money and property to family members. But to everyone who knew or felt they knew Yogi Berra, who died on Tuesday, September 22, at 90, he left much more.

In words, photos, videos and memorabilia, he left himself.

Outside the museum a bronze statue shows Yogi on one knee in his Yankee uniform with two bats, as if in the on-deck circle. Notice that he's not posing as the slugger he was; instead, he's looking up at the heavens, as if waiting for St. Peter to welcome him. Inside the museum, he's everywhere in his pride of accomplishment for someone who quit school after the eighth grade to work in a Pepsi-Cola bottling plant and at a shoe company. But nowhere is even the scent of ego.

It's not merely a museum. As its title says, it's also a learning center for thousands of bus-trip students and day-campers to appreciate values. Ambition and dedication, patriotism and integration, hard work and teamwork. It's all Yogi, just the way it happened.

Inside the entrance is the family photo: Yogi and his wife Carmen next to their three sons, daughters-in-law and grandchildren on a winding staircase in their Montclair home. Photos of young Lawrence Peter Berra's parents Pietro and Paulina (who called him "Lawdie"); his brothers Mike, Tony and John; his sister Josie; his pal Joe Garagiola, who lived across the street on The Hill in St. Louis; and their Stags A.C. sandlot teammates, one of whom gave him his "Yogi" nickname.

Over here is the D-Day exhibit. After playing for the Yankees farm team at Norfolk, Va., in the Class B Piedmont League in 1942, he enlisted in the Navy at 18 and volunteered for rocket-boat deployment. Off the Normandy beaches on June 6, 1944, he manned twin 50-caliber machine guns on a six-crew 36-foot LCSS (Landing Craft Support Small) as shipmates fired rockets at Nazi gun targets.

Nearby are some of Yogi's love letters. One evening in St. Louis after the war, he noticed a blonde waitress, Carmen Short, in Biggie's restaurant. As he traveled with the Yankees in 1947 and 1948, he wrote letters that she saved. "I will always love you as long as I live," one reads. "There never will be another girl but you. I love you, darling, more than ever. I sure hope you miss me as much as I miss you." They were married on January 26, 1949 in St. Ambrose Church.

Every few steps, his Yankee moments and teammates come alive. Meeting Babe Ruth as a rookie. Bill

Yogi Berra admiring his plaque in the Baseball Hall of Fame in Cooperstown after his induction in 1972. (AP Images)

Dickey "learning me his experience." Joe DiMaggio tousling his hair in a World Series celebration. Mickey Mantle. Whitey Ford. Phil Rizzuto. Roger Maris. Elston Howard. Billy Martin. The bronzed glove that he used to catch Don Larsen's perfect game. A replica of his Hall of Fame plaque. His 1954 and 1955 Most Valuable Player plaques; his 1951 plaque is in Cooperstown.

Framed, against a black-velvet background, are his 10 World Series championship rings as a player in all their diamonds-and-gold glory, each with a personal notation: '47 not bad, rookie. '49 first of five straight. '50 hit .322, 28 homers, 124 r.b.i. '51 first MVP season. '52 Bummer for Brooklyn. '53 unprecedented 5 in a row. '56 last Subway Series vs. Dodgers. '58 rallied to beat Milwaukee in WS. '61 one of 3 Yankee catchers with over 20 hrs. '62 at 37, winning never gets old.

On another wall, in a larger-than-life photo, Yogi is standing next to Gil Hodges, the Brooklyn Dodgers first baseman, during the 1955 World Series. Hodges is touching his face, which was grazed by a foul ball off his bat, as Yogi, in his catcher's gear, thoughtfully checks him. Years later, Yogi was a Mets coach when Hodges was hired to be the 1968 manager. When Hodges died in spring training in 1972, Yogi succeeded him, leading the Mets to the 1973 pennant.

Over here, on a far wall, George Steinbrenner is smiling somewhat sheepishly during his 1999 visit to the museum when he finally apologized for not personally telling Yogi that he was fired as manager in 1985—the insult that spurred Yogi's self-exile from Yankee Stadium for more than a decade. Not many people got the last word on the Yankees principal owner, but Yogi did.

On a video screen now, in a barber's chair in an Aflac commercial, Yogi is saying, "If you're hurt, it won't hurt to miss work. And they give you cash, which is just as good as money." And near the exit is the honest summation of all his Yogi-isms: "I really didn't say everything I said!" But in his final years, alluding to his pennant-race philosophy that "It ain't over till it's over," he often told friends that he wanted his tombstone to read, quite simply, "It's over."

Nice try, Yogi, but thanks to your museum and learning center, for you it never will be over. ∎

Yogi Berra tags out Phillies shortstop Granny Hamner at home on Oct. 7, 1950, during the Yankees' World Series–clinching Game 4 win, a victory aided by Berra's sixth-inning home run. (AP Images)

Carmen Berra, Yogi's Wife, Dies at 85

By Richard Sandomir • March 8, 2014

Carmen Berra, Yogi's companion for nearly 70 years, was one of the famous Yankees baseball wives who could be identified by their first name, like Eleanor (Gehrig), Merlyn (Mantle) and Cora (Rizzuto).

Carmen Berra, who died Friday at 85, met Yogi after the 1947 season at Biggie's steakhouse in St. Louis. She was a 19-year-old waitress and a local beauty. He had just played in 83 games for the Yankees in what amounted to his rookie season in the majors.

"I was bashful, nervous, not good-looking," Yogi wrote in one of his books. "I could hardly believe my luck that Carmen liked me as much as I liked her."

He romanced her with love letters from the road. They wed in early 1949 at St. Ambrose Church in St. Louis. Joe Garagiola was the best man. They formed a married team for 65 years, a union that produced 3 sons, 11 grandchildren and 1 great-grandson. They recently moved from their Montclair, N.J., home to an assisted-living facility.

In their own way, Yogi and Carmen were a boldface couple. She was among those at the Copacabana club in 1957 during a melee involving Yankee players and members of a bowling team who were heckling the entertainer Sammy Davis Jr.

When M. Donald Grant, the miserly Mets chairman, called the Berra home in 1975 to inform Yogi that he was to be fired as manager, Carmen asked for a two-week reprieve because her mother was visiting. Grant agreed.

And she was there, at Yogi's insistence, in the room at his museum in Little Falls, N.J., when George Steinbrenner apologized to him in 1999 for firing him as Yankees manager in 1985. ■

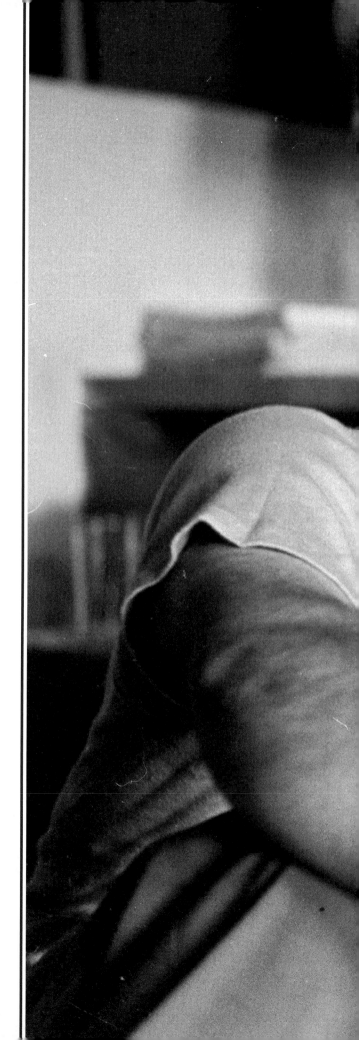

Yogi Berra getting a kiss from his wife, Carmen, before leaving for the clubhouse. (Getty Images)

From a '77 Spat, a Yankee Play

By Richard Sandomir • February 10, 2014

The central character in the new Broadway play "Bronx Bombers" is Yogi Berra. And why not? Yogi has been a Yankee, even when he was a Met, for nearly 70 years.

Creating a character like Yogi would be unlikely: a Hall of Fame catcher without an all-star physique, a beloved sage, a pitchman and the winning protagonist in a 14-year struggle for his dignity against George Steinbrenner. As a player, coach, manager or yogi-in-residence, he has been the human bridge to virtually every meaningful Yankee from Joe DiMaggio to Derek Jeter.

"I knew he was going to be an automatically empathetic character," said Eric Simonson, the playwright and director. "He's rich and dimensional, and he says all these great things, some of which he actually said, and he's the face of the Yankees.

The real Berra, now 88, has not seen the new production, but he and his wife, Carmen, attended its Off Broadway version last year.

"He laughed his butt off watching it," said Lindsay Berra, the oldest of his 11 grandchildren. "Grandpa likes to laugh, and he can laugh at himself. And my grandmother loved the choice of clothing for her and her glasses."

The play centers on Berra's distress over the feud that erupted when Yankees manager Billy Martin yanked Reggie Jackson out of right field for apparently loafing on a fly ball in a game against the Red Sox in Fenway Park in June 1977. Before a full brawl between them could begin in the dugout, Berra and Elston Howard, two of Martin's coaches, held the combatants apart.

As played by Peter Scolari, Berra tries to broker a cease-fire between the two in his hotel room, where Martin is agitated and weepy, and Jackson is full of swagger and the "immensity" of himself. Still unsettled, Berra hallucinates that Babe Ruth is speaking to him.

There is, of course, considerable dramatic license in all this, especially in Berra's dream that he and Carmen are the hosts at a dinner party of pin-striped royalty with Ruth, Howard, DiMaggio, Jeter, Lou Gehrig and Mickey Mantle.

It is a "Field of Dreams"–like encounter in the Berras' home in Montclair, N.J., without the cornfield.

Lindsay Berra said that the play captured the spirit of the characters, the sweetness of her grandparents' love story and the look of Carmen Berra.

"When Tracy comes out in the little tweed suit with the straight blond bob, I burst out in tears, she looked so much like Grammy," she said, referring to Tracy Shayne. "At one point, she put her hands on her chest, and with her nude-colored manicure, it was so Grammy. The hairs on my back stood up." ∎

Peter Scolari and Tracy Shayne as Yogi and Carmen Berra in the play "Bronx Bombers." (AP Images)

1

The Hill

Incubator of Baseball Talent

By David Waldstein • October 20, 2011

ST. LOUIS—Few cities resonate with as much baseball tradition as St. Louis, and few seem as doused in team colors as this city, where even the downtown fountains are spraying water tinted Cardinal rouge this October.

Some of the best teams and players in the sport's history have played in St. Louis, at Sportsman's Park, Robison Field and the two Busch Stadiums. And the game echoes in other parts of the city, too, particularly in a neighborhood called The Hill, which is seven miles from downtown.

It was there, on a vacant lot on Elizabeth Avenue, that two sons of Italian immigrants honed their soccer, football and, more than anything else, baseball skills.

One of them was Lawrence Berra, who later became known nationwide as Yogi, and the other was Joe Garagiola. They were still babies when the Cardinals won their first World Series in 1926. Each is now a baseball elder whose name endures.

"We played all the time," Berra said in a telephone interview Thursday as he recalled the neighborhood in which he grew up. "We would go right after school and play until the 4:30 factory whistle. That's when our fathers got off work and we had to go home and open a can of beer. Then it was back outside to play."

Today, the Elizabeth Avenue lot has been replaced by a house, but the same homes that Berra and Garagiola grew up in still stand, directly across the street from one another at 5447 and 5446 Elizabeth Avenue.

A niece of Berra's, Mary Frances Brown, still lives in the old family home, now renovated.

In fact, much of The Hill's orderly working-class streets, homes and shops remain intact, not all that much changed from an era when sons of Italian immigrants became Americanized, often through sports.

Elizabeth Avenue has been renamed Hall of Fame Place, and sidewalk plaques mark the homes of Berra and Garagiola, and the legendary announcer Jack Buck, who bought a house down the block at the corner of Elizabeth and Macklind when he was broadcasting Cardinals games.

There are also plaques in front of the homes of five members of the United States soccer team, which upset England in the 1950 World Cup.

Like everyone in the area, Berra and Garagiola grew up worshiping the Cardinals, but only Garagiola was fortunate enough to be signed by the team. He went on to play six seasons with the Cardinals and was a catcher on the 1946 club that beat Ted Williams and the Boston Red Sox to win the World Series.

Although Berra was overlooked by the Cardinals and the other local team, the St. Louis Browns, he managed to do all right. He signed with the Yankees in 1943, won 10 World Series and three Most Valuable Player awards, played 19 seasons in all and was elected to the Hall of Fame in 1972.

But he said Thursday that his older brother Tony, nicknamed Lefty for his slugging power from the left side, was the better player.

"My father wouldn't let him or my other brothers Mike and John play," Berra said. "He didn't know about baseball. They had to go to work and get a paycheck. But you ask anyone up on The Hill: Tony was the best."

Yogi Berra focuses before a 1959 preseason game against the Cardinals (John G. Zimmerman/Getty Images)

The Hill remains an Italian neighborhood, with St. Ambrose Church, which Berra and Garagiola attended, still a focal point for the residents.

The numerous Italian restaurants and shops, the presence of Milo's Bocce Garden, where people can gather for a beer and a game of bocce, evoke a time when Italian was the predominant language spoken in the streets and where workingmen's hands were calloused from their labors at the nearby clay mines, brick factories and spaghetti plants.

"You go to a lot of Italian neighborhoods in a lot of American cities and you ask, 'Where are the Italians?'" said Joe DeGregorio, a second-generation Italian-American who runs tours of the neighborhood.

Not in The Hill, though. DeGregorio said that when immigration began here in the latter part of the 19th century, many people arrived from a cluster of five towns outside Milan in northern Italy, rather than from Sicily and the south, the source of so many other Italian immigrants to the United States.

Clara Scozzari, 85, still lives on Elizabeth Avenue, near where she grew up. She has known Berra, she says, virtually all of her life, or since they both attended Shaw's School.

"They used to play baseball in the street, and we would watch sometimes," Scozzari said. "He would act tough, but in the end he was always very nice."

There is still a large population of Italian immigrants in The Hill, people like Giovanni Dominic Galati, the owner of Dominic's restaurant.

"It's a place where you can walk to the bakery and get a loaf of bread," Galati said. "And after work, have a beer at Milo's and play bocce, go to church and walk home. It's still a very unique place."

Eight decades ago, it was where Garagiola and Berra played sandlot games. ■

The family home where Yogi Berra grew up, at 5447 Elizabeth Ave. in the St. Louis Hill neighborhood, is shown in a Nov. 13, 1957 photo. (Getty Images)

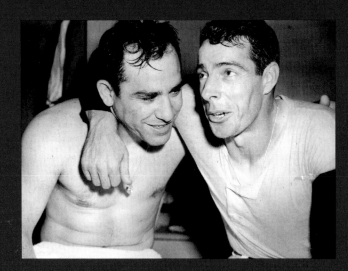

Yogi Berra in Unfamiliar Role

By Glenn Collins • February 15, 2000

Finally, the French Government got the chance to present its Normandy-Beach medal to a D-Day veteran who couldn't attend the 50th-anniversary celebration in 1994. Former Seaman First Class Yogi Berra, who at the age of 18 manned a 36-foot rocket boat off Omaha Beach, was presented yesterday with the Medaille du Jubile in a brief ceremony at the institution that bears his name, the Yogi Berra Museum and Learning Center in Little Falls, New Jersey.

The French had to pursue the 74-year-old Mr. Berra "because I don't publicize that I was there," he said. Mr. Berra was so moved by the presentation of the bronze medal that he uttered not one zenlike Yogi-ism. But he did express relief that, at the medal-pinning ceremony, "they didn't give me any French kisses." ∎

Above: Yogi Berra and Joe DiMaggio celebrate winning the 1950 World Series against the Philadelphia Phillies. (Photo by Sporting News/ Sporting News via Getty Images)
Opposite: Berra swings away. (Getty Images)

2

Yankees Player

Bombers Overcome Tars, 19-5

By John Drebinger • April 8, 1947

NORFOLK, Va., April 7—Looks as though something will have to be done about this Yogi Berra and very soon the burden of the task will rest with the seven other clubs in the American League.

For today this amazing little fellow, whom manager Bucky Harris on a starry night in Caracas converted from a chunky catcher into a chunky outfielder of even more extraordinary proportions, again grabbed all the spotlight as the Yankees belted Buddy Hassett's Norfolk farm hands into submission, 19 to 5.

With a homer, a single with the bases full, and sundry other accomplishments, Yogi, who alone seems totally unaware of the commotion stirring all around him, hammered in six tallies for the Bombers who were making this their next to the last stop on their journey home.

Berra seemed determined to stop at nothing. His homer, a tremendous clout with two aboard in the first inning, was his third in two days and fourth of spring training. His single in the second with the bases full drove in two more tallies. Actually it cleared the sacks, for the shot also went through the opposing rightfielder, so terrifying are the blows that zoom off the Yogi bludgeon these days. Later on he rattled a two-bagger off the rightfield fence.

The Berra homer, incidentally, was one of the longest shots ever seen in this park. It cleared a high barrier in almost dead center, 450 feet from home plate.

The shot drew tremendous applause from every quarter but the Yankee bench, where Yogi's teammates continue to rib him by greeting his every outstanding achievement with a stony silence. ■

Yanks Clinch Flag, Aided by Reynolds No-Hitter

By John Drebinger • September 29, 1951

In a brilliant display of all-around skill that included a nerve-tingling no-hitter in one encounter and a seven-run explosion in the other, the Yankees yesterday clinched the 1951 American League pennant. It was their third flag in a row and 18th in 30 years.

With Allie Reynolds tossing his second no-hitter of the year—a feat previously achieved by only one other hurler in history—the Bombers vanquished the Red Sox in the opener of the double-header at the Stadium, 8 to 0.

Then, behind big Vic Raschi, the Stengeleers crushed the already eliminated Bosox, 11 to 3, to the cheers of 39,038 fans. Joe DiMaggio further embellished the triumph with a three-run homer as another flag was nailed to the Yankee masthead.

Those who sat in on the show are not likely to forget those last tense moments when Reynolds, who had walked four batters during the game, had to collect "twenty-eight outs" before reaching his goal.

With two outs in the ninth and the still-fearsome Ted Williams at bat, a high foul was struck back of home plate. Yogi Berra, usually sure on these, scampered under it but in the next agonizing moment the

Yogi Berra, as he was often seen, taking it all in from behind the mask. (Sam Falk/The New York Times)

ball squirmed out of his glove as the Yanks' chunky backstop went sprawling on his face.

It meant Williams would have to be pitched to some more. But Reynolds, an amazingly good-natured competitor under the most trying circumstances, patted Berra consolingly on the back and said, "Don't worry, Yogi, we'll get him again."

And sure enough, up went another high, twisting foul off to the right side of the plate. It looked tougher than the first one. But Yogi meant to catch this one if it burst a girth rope and as he finally froze the ball directly in front of the Yankee dugout, Reynolds first, and virtually all the other Yankees jubilantly piled on top of him. For a moment, it looked as if Berra, not Reynolds, was the hero of the occasion. ■

Berra Is Selected as Most Valuable in American League

By Joseph M. Sheehan • November 9, 1951

Lawrence Peter (Yogi) Berra, durable and hard-hitting catcher of the World Series champion Yankees, yesterday was named the American League's most valuable player of 1951.

In one of the closest polls ever conducted by the Baseball Writers Association of America, the stocky 26-year-old receiver of the Bombers edged out Ned Garver, the St. Louis Browns' pitcher, and Allie Reynolds, his Yankee battery-mate.

The voting panel of three writers from each of the eight American League cities gave six first-place votes each to Berra, Garver, and Reynolds. However, Yogi had the strongest support in the weighted scoring of each writer's first ten selections.

Berra tallied 184 points to 157 for Garver, a 20-game winner with the last-place Browns, and 125 for Reyn-

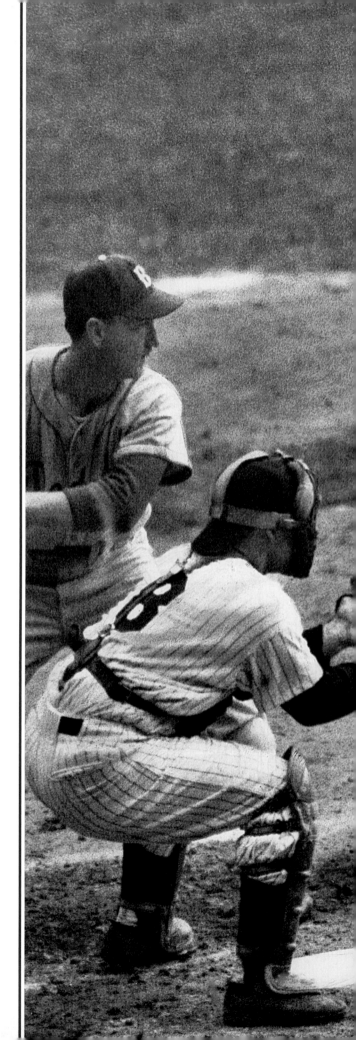

Jackie Robinson steals home during the opening game of the World Series on September 28, 1955. Yogi Berra erupted after Robinson was called safe, and for the rest of his life would assure anyone who mentioned the play that Robinson was out. (Meyer Liebowitz/The New York Times)

olds, first American League pitcher to hurl two no-hitters in one season.

Five other players received first-place mention. They were Orestes Minoso, Chicago's rookie outfielder, who placed fourth with 120 points; Ferris Fain, Philadelphia's league batting leader, sixth with 103 points; Ellis Kinder, Boston's relief ace, seventh with 66 points; Phil Rizzuto, Yankee shortstop, who won last year's award and finished eleventh this time with 47 points; and Ed Lopat, Yankee southpaw, twelfth with 44 points.

The selection of Berra marked the first time that catchers were picked as the most valuable player of both major leagues. Roy Campanella, Brooklyn's slugging backstop, last week won the National League award.

Mickey Cochrane, named in 1928 and 1934, was the only other catcher to receive the American League award.

Winning the most valuable player designation is an old Yankee habit. As the 10th Bomber since the poll became official in 1922, Berra joins such illustrious predecessors as Babe Ruth (1923), Lou Gehrig (1927 and 1936), Joe DiMaggio (1936, 1941, and 1947), Joe Gordon (1942), Spud Chandler (1943), and Rizzuto (1950).

By his own standards, Berra did not have his best season in 1951. A September slump dropped his batting average to .294, as against .322 in 1950. And though he led the Yankees in these respects, his 27 home runs and 88 runs batted in fell short of his corresponding 1950 totals of 28 and 124.

However, he was the solid man of the Yankees on a day-to-day basis. Besides being their most dangerous hitter and a fine base-runner, Berra did a remarkable job behind the bat. He caught 141 games.

To Yogi's astute handling of his pitchers belongs a good share of credit for the 24 shutouts turned in by the Yankee staff. This was the biggest whitewashing job in

World Series line-up for Yankees chosen by Casey Stengel, right, in dugout. From left are Roger Maris, Yogi Berra, Mickey Mantle, Bobby Richardson, Bill Skowron, Tony Kubek, Art Ditmnar, Hector Lopez and Cletis Boyer. (Ernie Sisto/The New York Times)

the American League since the Red Sox accounted for 26 shut-outs in the "dead ball" days of 1918.

At the handsome new home in Woodcliff Lake, New Jersey, to which he moved from St. Louis this spring with his wife, Carmen, and two young children, Berra received the news of his selection with pleased surprise.

"I never thought I'd get it," said Yogi, over the phone. "I'm sure tickled pink, though, and I feel great about it." ∎

Berra Signs Yanks' Contract

By Roscoe McGowen • November 4, 1954

Lawrence Peter (Yogi) Berra yesterday signed a one-year contract with the New York Yankees for a salary estimated at $48,000, making him the highest-paid catcher in baseball and "probably" the highest-paid Yankee for 1955, according to George Weiss, general manager.

"We haven't mailed out our contracts yet," said Weiss, "but I'd say Berra has a good chance to be the top man."

The affable and outspoken Yogi described his negotiations with Weiss thus:

"We were at the Grantland Rice dinner last Sunday night and Weiss asked me what I wanted next year. I told him I didn't want to name a figure. I said: 'You name one and maybe I'll like it.' He named one and I said: 'Okay.' That's all there was to it.

"Did I get a raise?" He grinned broadly. "Sure, I got a good raise."

Somebody asked Yogi how much he was paid on his first contract in the organization when he signed with Norfolk, Virginia (Piedmont League). Yogi hesitated and turned to Weiss.

"Shall I tell 'em?" he asked.

"Sure, why not?" answered Weiss.

With an almost embarrassed grin Yogi said, "Ninety"—meaning $90 per month.

Joe DiMaggio greets Yogi Berra at the plate after Berra belts a home run in the sixth inning of Game 4 of the World Series. (Getty Images)

"But," Weiss hastily interposed, "we gave Yogi a $500 bonus to sign."

So Berra, baseball's top catcher in 1954, has jumped from $90 to approximately $9,000 a month in thirteen years (including next year), which must be rated as reasonable financial progress.

Yogi had one of his better years in the recent season, batting .307 and driving in 125 runs, the latter his top figure in his eight full seasons with the Yankees. His hits included twenty-seven doubles, six triples and twenty-two home runs.

Berra, who won't be 30 years old until next May 12, caught in 149 games, including many double-headers, and played third base in the season's final game.

Yogi's best hitting year was in 1950 with a .322 average and his top home run season was in 1952, when he belted thirty. In 1950 Yogi drove in 124 runs.

"I got the minimum, $5,000, the first year," he said. "Then I got a $4,000 raise every year except one, when I got a $5,000 boost. After that," he added impishly, "you're on your own."

It was, of course, after his big 1950 season that the increases began to jump rapidly. For the 1954 season he probably was getting considerably more than the estimates of $40,000 to $42,000, which were made last winter. ∎

Berra Chosen MVP for Second Time

By Roscoe McGowen • December 10, 1954

Yogi Berra, the Yankees' catcher, yesterday won the American League's Most Valuable Player Award for the second time.

"Winning this one is a bigger thrill than winning it in 1951," Berra said.

Yogi is the sixth two-time winner in his league and the first repeater since Ted Williams won in 1946 and

Whitey Ford and Yogi Berra leave Yankee Stadium after signing their new contracts for the 1957 season. (Ernie Sisto/The New York Times)

1949. There have been two triple winners—Jimmy Foxx in 1932, 1933, and 1938 and Joe DiMaggio in 1939, 1941, and 1947.

The double, winners were Hank Greenberg, 1935 and 1940; Hal Newhouser, 1944 and 1945; and Williams.

The vote by the twenty-four-man committee of the Baseball Writers Association of America was close. Berra outscored two Cleveland players—Larry Doby and Bobby Avila.

Yogi polled 230 points to 210 for Doby, an outfielder; and 203 for Avila, a second baseman. The Yankee catcher was named on seven first-place ballots, while Doby, Avila, and Bob Lemon, Indian pitcher, attracted five each. Minnie Minoso of the White Sox was the only other player to gain first-place support, with two votes.

This division of voting on Cleveland players tipped the scales in Berra's favor. Three other Indians also figured in the balloting. Al Rosen, last year's unanimous winner, polled 16 points, Mike Garcia 6, and Jim Hegan 5.

Aside from Berra, only four Yankees made the list and none drew a first-place ballot. Bob Grim, 20-game winning rookie pitcher, was eleventh with 25 points. The outfielders, Mickey Mantle and Irv Noren, tied with 16 points, and Hank Bauer got 4.

Berra was a solid man on the Yankees despite their failure to win the pennant. He batted .307 and drove in 125 runs, one behind Doby, the league leader. Yogi's 179 hits in 584 times at bat included 22 home runs. ■

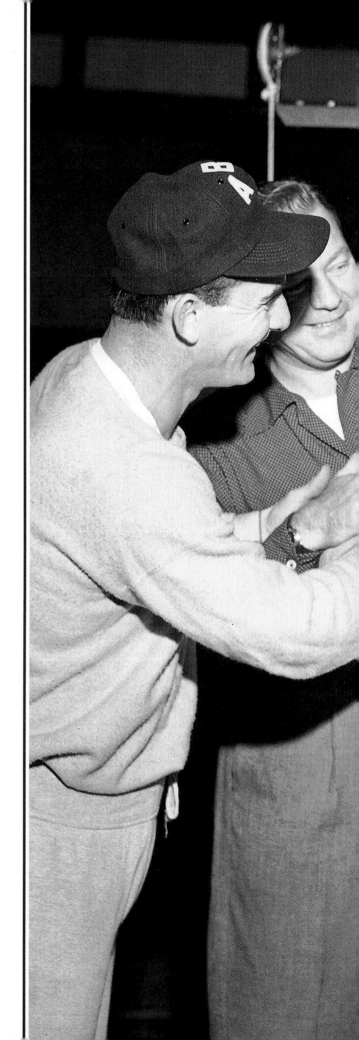

Yogi Berra gets a thumping congratulations after learning that he'll be named the 1951 American League MVP. From Left to right are Sid Gordon, Ed Lopat, Berra, Gil Hodges, and Gil McDougald. (AP Images)

Berra is Named Most Valuable in League Again

By John Drebinger • December 4, 1955

CHICAGO—Yogi Berra, a potent factor in the seven pennants the Yankees have won in the last nine campaigns, again has been named the American League's most valuable player.

The Bombers' stout-hearted and strong-armed catcher was declared the winner today of the 24-man committee of the Baseball Writers Association of America that decided the disposition of the Kenesaw Mountain Landis Trophy for 1955.

The election, however, was a tight one. Yogi finished on top with 218 points. Second place went to Al Kaline, the Detroit Tigers' slugging young outfielder and the season's American League batting champion.

Naturally, I'm very happy," Berra said. "I thought I had a chance, but figured Al Kaline might beat me out."

Berra thus becomes the third player in American League history to win the award three times. Jimmy Foxx, powerful home run clouter of the then–Philadelphia Athletics, won it in 1932 and 1933 and again in 1938 as a member of the Boston Red Sox.

That mark was not equaled until Joe DiMaggio, the Yankee Clipper, came along to win the prize in 1939, 1941, and 1947. Berra gained his previous crowns in 1951 and 1954. Only one other player, besides Foxx and Berra, has won the award in two successive years. The Tigers' Hal Newhouser made it in 1944 and 1945.

The 30-year-old Berra has been a New York stalwart since 1947. In the ensuing years he has compiled a lifetime batting average of .293, with a total of 308 home runs and 898 runs batted in for an even 1,200 games. Last season, catching 147 games, Yogi's batting mark slipped to .272, his lowest since he entered the majors.

But there was no denying he was still the great driving force of the American League champions, their most dependable clutch hitter, in addition to being an almost flawless receiver. He hit 27 homers and drove in 108 runs to make 1955 his fourth year over the 100 mark. ■

Commissioner Ford Frick, left, presents Yogi Berra the Judge Kenesaw Landis Memorial plaque as the 1955 American League MVP at Yankee Stadium on April 20, 1956, with manager Casey Stengel at the presentation. (AP Photo)

Catching Perfection

By Yogi Berra • May 22, 1998

Not many days go by that I'm not reminded about Don Larsen's perfect game in the 1956 World Series, 42 years ago. People always ask me about it, and now it's sort of like deja vu again after David Wells's perfect game for the Yankees last Sunday. It's something that was so magical, it kinda lives on forever. Next to getting in the Hall of Fame in 1972, it was probably my greatest thrill in baseball.

Don had to pitch the game, I had to call it. As a catcher, you take responsibility for every pitch (except for the one that hits a batter in the back and starts a brawl—that's just a pitcher losing his head). You have to know early on what's working for a pitcher. Larsen had a good fastball and curve and slider, just like Wells. Can you believe those guys came from the same high school? Anyway, Larsen threw 97 pitches and didn't shake me off once.

It's not always so easy, because pitchers think they're so smart all the time. You have to handle each one differently. You have to know which guys you holler at, which guys you just pet.

Allie Reynolds, even when he threw those two no-hitters in 1951, would try to get too cute with a big lead. Vic Raschi, you had to get on him. I'd yell at him, "Pitching for 20 years and you still can't get the ball over." And he'd yell back, "Get back behind the plate you..." finishing the sentence off with a word that can't be printed here.

Bob Turley was the opposite. He was a little wild, and I'd just pet him by saying, "You're better than that." When Whitey Ford would throw those slow curves on 3–0, I'd lose it and let him hear about it. I'd really let him hear about it.

Larsen was a little different. You had to get on him a little bit. Remember that Ol' Gooney Bird—that's what we called him—had a good year for us and could throw with the best of them, but sometimes his mind wasn't in the game. In that same World Series, Casey Stengel pulled

Don Larsen wraps his arms around Yogi Berra after the final pitch of Game 5 of the 1956 World Series against the Brooklyn Dodgers at Yankee Stadium. Larsen pitched the first perfect game in World Series history as the Yankees defeated Sal Maglie and the Dodgers, 2-0. (Getty Images)

him in the second inning of Game 2 because he got behind a lot of those Dodger hitters and walked four batters.

But in Game 5, he had the best control of any pitcher I'd ever seen. I knew all the Dodgers—Pee Wee, Campy, Furillo, Hodges—and was saying something to them when they got to the plate, like I always did. None of the Dodgers said much back. I remember Carl Furillo saying, "Larsen has really good stuff today," and I just nodded.

By the ninth inning, I couldn't talk to anyone—my heart was pounding. I was just hoping Larsen wouldn't make a mistake, and he didn't. I felt like a kid on Christmas morning when the final strike was called for the last out. It's funny, leaping into a pitcher's arms is something I'd never done before. Once I jumped on Bob Kuzava after he saved the 1952 Series for us, but he had his back turned.

A perfect game is incredible, but one in the World Series is a miracle, and I'll always cherish it. Right after the game, I had Pete Sheehy, our equipment manager, bronze my catcher's mitt. It's one of my most treasured possessions, and it's going right in that museum they're building for me in Montclair. Like I said, perfect games kinda live forever. ■

Yanks Champions as Berra Hits Two

By John Drebinger • October 11, 1956

After a solid week of thrills, the 1956 World Series ended yesterday in an old and familiar pattern.

The Yankees, whose virtual monopoly of the world championship had been interrupted last October, roared back to reclaim their laurels in a welter of superlative performances.

Casey Stengel's Bombers crushed the Dodgers in the seventh and deciding game at Ebbets Field, 9 to 0, before a gathering of 33,782.

It was a loud and emphatic vindication. It violently reversed last October's struggle, when Walter Alston's Brooks bagged the seventh game to capture Brooklyn's first series title.

Four home runs, the last a grand slam, fired behind the brilliant three-hit pitching of 23-year-old Johnny Kucks, wrapped up this one. The amazing American League champions gained their 17th World Series title and sixth under the leadership of Charles Dillon Stengel.

The incomparable Yogi Berra exploded the first two Yankee homers, each with a runner aboard. The first was hit in the first inning, the second in the third.

Berra, driving in four runs, wound up with 10 runs batted in for the Series. That topped by one the record the late Lou Gehrig had set with the Yanks in 1928.

When Bill Skowron cleared the sacks in the seventh, it marked the first time two grand slams had been hit in one Series. Berra had hit a four-run homer in the second game. Only six have been hit in history. ■

Berra Voted into Hall of Fame

By Joseph Durso • January 20, 1972

Sandy Koufax, Yogi Berra, and Early Wynn were elected to baseball's Hall of Fame yesterday in the heaviest voting in the 35-year history of the poll.

In a landslide, Koufax led the rest with 344 of the 396 votes cast by the Baseball Writers Association of America. It was the highest total ever received by a player and, at the age of 36, the former pitching star of the Brooklyn and Los Angeles Dodgers also became the youngest elected. He also joined a select group of nine who made it the first year they had become eligible—five years after retirement.

Berra, for 18 seasons a catcher with the Yankees, made it on his second attempt with 339 votes. Wynn, a 300-game winner on the mound with Washington, Cleveland, and the Chicago White Sox, made it on his fourth with 301. To be elected, they had to be mentioned on 75 percent of the ballots, in this case 297.

For Berra, who was named Lawrence Peter after his birth 46 years ago in St. Louis, the voting reversed a disappointment suffered a year ago, when he fell 28 votes short.

"I thought maybe I'd make it this year," he said. "Even a great player like Joe DiMaggio didn't make it

Yogi Berra waits for the pitch during a 1956 game at Yankee Stadium. (Getty Images)

in his first year. But whenever you make it, it's a great thrill. I got four or five phone calls from friends this morning, and I had to tell them I didn't know anything yet, even though I did."

During his 20-year career as a player, Berra batted .285, chiefly as the catcher on the great Yankee teams of the 1950s; hit 358 home runs; and appeared in 14 All-Star Games and 14 World Series.

He also was manager of the Yankees in 1964, was dropped after they lost the Series, switched to the Mets, played briefly with them and has been their first-base coach the last six seasons.

He was short and squat, and became part of folklore. But in uniform he was all business. He once went 148 games without an error, handling 950 chances cleanly. He has hit more home runs than any other catcher, and holds 10 Series records. ■

Manager Berra Ends Assault on Records by Player Berra

October 25, 1963

Yogi Berra broke two records merely by lining out in his only appearance as a player during the 1963 World Series.

The new Yankee manager raised his record of total Series games to 75 and his total of Series at-bats to 259.

Aside from his many Series marks, Berra holds the major league record for a catcher in home runs with 313 (with 45 as an outfielder), in consecutive chances without an error, 950, and in consecutive games without an error, 148.

He tied a major league record by leading American League catchers in double plays six times and tied an American League mark for home runs in a season by a catcher with 30.

Yogi played in 2,116 games for the Yankees, second only to Lou Gehrig's 2,164. He was selected the American League's Most Valuable Player in 1951, 1954, and 1955. He was the first player to hit a pinch-homer in the World Series, connecting against the Brooklyn Dodgers October 2, 1947. He is still one of only nine players in Series history to have hit a pinch-homer. ■

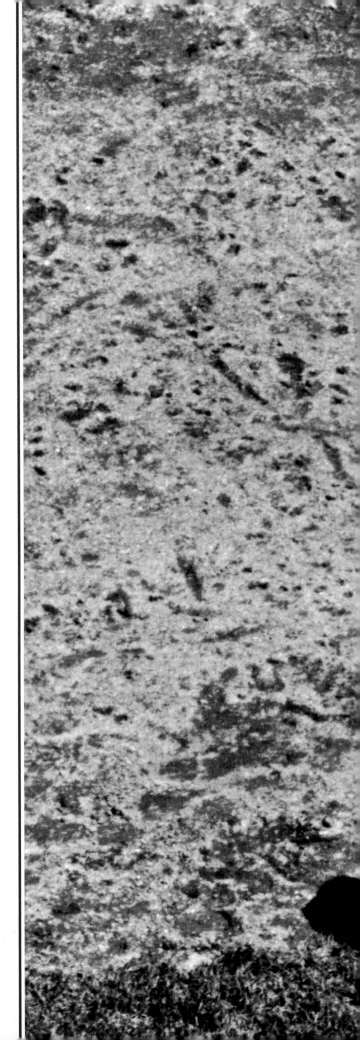

Yogi Berra looks up as he gets under a foul pop-up during a game at Yankee Stadium. (Getty Images)

WORLD SERIES RECORDS SET

- Most Series played—14
- Most times on, winning club—10
- Most games, total Series—75
- Most at-bats, total Series—259
- Most runs, total Series—41
- Most runs batted in, total Series—39
- Most hits, total Series—71
- Most singles, total Series—49
- Most total bases, total Series—117
- Most Series, one or more runs batted in, total Series—11.
- Most games caught, total Series—63.
- Highest fielding average, catcher, seven-game Series—1.000, 66 chances (1958)
- Most putouts, catcher, seven-game Series—60 (1958)
- Most putouts, catcher, total Series—421
- Most assists, catcher, total Series—36
- Most chances accepted, catcher, seven-game Series—66 (1952 and 1958)
- Most chances accepted, catcher, total Series—457
- Most double plays, catcher, total Series—6

WORLD SERIES RECORDS TIED

- One of 15 to hit two home runs in Series game, (Oct. 10, 1956)
- One of nine to hit home run as pinch-hitter (Oct. 2, 1947)
- One of eight to hit grand-slam homer (Oct. 5, 1956)
- Most runs batted in one inning—4
- Most times hit by pitched ball in game—2 (Oct. 2, 1953)
- Made one or more base hits in each game of seven-game Series (1955)
- Most doubles, total Series—10 (1957 and 1958)
- Played seven-game Series without striking out
- Most times hit by pitched ball, total Series—3
- Most long hits, total Series—22

Yogi Berra being congratulated by Roger Maris, left, and the bat boy after hitting a home run. (Ernie Sisto/The New York Times)

3

Yankees Manager 1963-1964

Yankees Sign Berra to Manager

By John Drebinge • October 25, 1963

Amid all the fanfare usually reserved for a visiting potentate, Lawrence Peter (Yogi) Berra was named yesterday as manager of the New York Yankees.

In the same plush Savoy-Hilton setting where three years ago Casey Stengel and George Weiss departed as manager and general manager, respectively, Yogi took over.

It was strictly Yogi's party, which means it was quite unlike anything seen before. In fact, there were times when it was difficult to tell Yogi from the milling cameramen, reporters, and newsreel operators.

Right off, the 38-year-old Berra, of whom an observer once said, "He doesn't even look like a Yankee," set some sort of record. He became perhaps the first star baseball player to take a cut in salary to become a manager.

Yogi succeeded Ralph Houk who, after winning three straight pennants as Stengel's successor, moved up last Tuesday to general manager, replacing Roy Hamey. Yogi signed for only one year and a salary reputed to be $35,000.

The one-year contract, said the club president, Dan Topping, in making the announcement, was strictly Yogi's idea.

"Berra is receiving the same salary," said Topping, "as was given to Stengel and Houk in their first year as manager."

In his career as a player, during which for more a decade he ranked as one of baseball's greatest catchers, Yogi is understood to have received a top salary of $55,000. In 1963, serving as a part-time catcher, pinch-hitter, and first-base coach, Yogi received $45,000. So to take the new job, he's taking a cut. Shrewd Yogi, however, had his reasons.

Why did he insist on a one-year contract? Yogi explained that he wanted to decide for himself whether he was making good.

"If I feel I can't do the job," said Yogi, "I don't want to stay managing. I want to get a taste of it. If I can't do it, I'll quit. If I can," he added with a smile and a sly look in Topping's direction, "I'll stick round a while and we can talk about a new contract."

Yogi then announced his retirement as a player. He won't even stay on the active list as a pinch-hitter.

"Managing, I think, is tough enough of a job," said Yogi. "Of course, if something should happen and my bosses think I should go back as a player, I would do it. But right now I don't have any such plans." ∎

Yogi Berra grins as Yankees general manager Roy Hamey points to a blackboard which confirms the rumors of Berra's new status on Jan. 17, 1963. Though the rumors of the assignment have been going the rounds for a week and Berra has known about it for a month, it is now official that he will be a playing coach. He will coach at first base when he isn't playing, according to Hamey. (AP Images)

Catchers
Howard
Blanchard
Berra!

NEW PLAYER
COACH
BERRA!!

Casey's Little Helper

By Arthur Daley • October 25, 1963

Back in the old days Casey Stengel use a flippant reference whenever he spoke of his favorite ballplayer, Yogi Berra. Ol' Case didn't first-name him or last-name him.

"Mister Berra, which helps me manage the Yankees," Casey used to say.

Yesterday the Yankees gave Yogi a do-it-yourself kit and formally installed him as their manager. Thus does the most prized post in big-league baseball go to an untried operative whose public image has been that of a buffoon. But his private image long has been one of sagaciousness, intuitive intelligence, and warmth, of a man with sweeping knowledge of his trade. Once before the Bombers made a move quite similar to this one—when they named Stengel. They did not regret it. They may not regret this one, either.

Man of Poise

Yogi made a tremendously favorable impression at his coronation ceremony. The man who once was at a total loss for words when hauled before a microphone handled himself with poise and distinction. He was wearing a sheepish look when he entered the room for his first press conference as Yankee manager. But he glanced around, saw only the smiling faces of his press-box buddies, and relaxed. He was perfectly natural and merely turned on the charm. It is irresistible.

"When they first tol' me about this," he said, grinning like a gargoyle, "I almost flipped."

He won the hearts of his listeners with his brightly spoken straight answers and won them still more when he lapsed once into what has come to known as a Berraism. It emerged when he talked about the way he tried to prepare himself all last season when he knew he would inherit the managerial job.

"You can observe a lot by watchin'," said Yogi. It was a remark worthy of the old master himself, Stengel.

It was quite a revelation to see Yogi on his feet, fielding questions with the same skill used in fielding baseballs. Here are samples:

Why has he retired as a player? "There's enough trouble managin' the ball club."

What's his biggest problem? "If I can manage."

What makes a good manager? "A good ball club."

Are you a softie? "To a certain extent."

The Big Question

The last answer is the most important. The easy-going, good-natured Yogi is far and away the best-liked ballplayer this side of Stan Musial. He has no enemies and it's almost impossible to fault him or his cheerful disposition—up to now anyway. So enormous has been his popularity that even rookies will kid him. Veterans take that for granted.

When the Yankee regulars reported at Fort Lauderdale last spring, Yogi had been in camp for weeks in his new role as coach. On the first day the ineffable Berra gravitated toward his pals—Whitey Ford and Mickey Mantle.

"Hey, Whitey," said Yogi after practice, "let's you and me go out to eat together tonight. Mickey, too."

"Nothing doing," said Whitey with feigned coldness. "You can't eat with the fellers any more. You're a coach now."

"Officers don't eat with the enlisted men," said Mantle.

"Aw, come on, fellers," wailed Yogi. They finally condescended to let him join them.

The quick-witted Ford is the needler supreme and he never could resist giving jabs to the usually vulnerable Yogi. Nor was there ever much resistance by the other Yankees.

Yogi Berra flashes a giant smile as he holds the ball pitched to him in his 2,000th major league game on

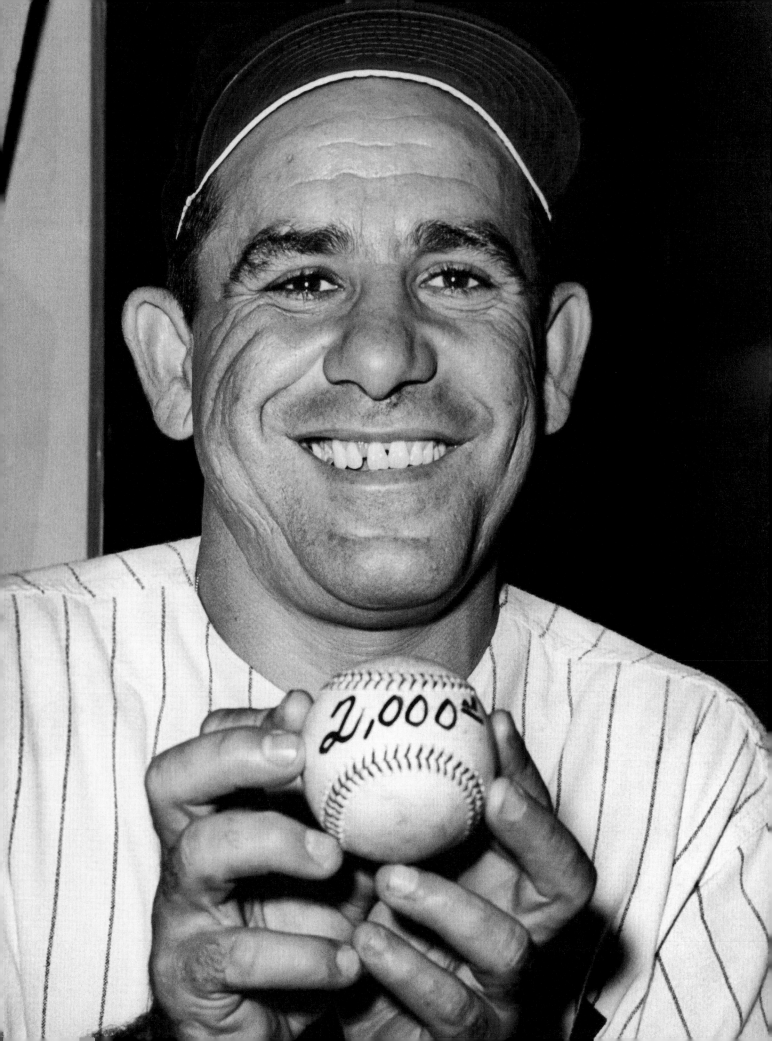

The Whip-Snapper

Yogi is a softie, and Frank Frisch once declared, "A good manager has to have a bit of a louse in him." Discipline will be Berra's chief problem because there's no louse in him at all. The players respect him highly as a baseball man and now they will have to broaden it into respecting him as a person. A firm hand and a quick snap of the whip in the beginning could settle that situation in a hurry.

"I know players and their habits," said Yogi with total unconcern.

That inside information should be a help. In fact, Berra has a wider knowledge of all baseball personnel than any other man in the sport and he has forgotten nothing he ever learned.

No man will begin a career with more fervent wishes for success than Lawrence Peter Berra. Such popularity must be deserved. ■

Lovable Myth and Sensitive Man

By Robert Lipsyte • October 25, 1963

The hydrant-shaped folk hero called Yogi Berra is a cuddly noble savage who lusts after comic books, innocently scratches himself in public, loves children and dogs, exudes natural humor, and swings down from his tree house to excel in a game he would happily play for nothing.

Yesterday Yogi, the inspiration for a cartoon animal (Yogi Bear), was named manager of the New York Yankees.

The man named Lawrence Peter Berra, however, was once a poor little boy taunted for his stumpy ugliness, a teenager who had to leave the ninth grade because his family needed money, a coal-yard laborer who saved money with banana-and-mustard sandwiches.

The myth and the man are never very far apart: Both are short, dark, hairy, with a lined and scarred face, short, muscular arms, and the waddling gait of one who is balancing slippery weights on his shoulders.

Yogi Berra autographs some baseballs as his son, Larry, watches. (Larry C. Morris/The New York Times)

Both have hit a lot a home runs, caught many fine games, earned a great deal of money, and made reams of comical remarks. But like all myths, the one called Yogi was created by the needs of other people.

A Man You Can't Hate

First of all, the myth is lovable because people can never hate a man they can laugh at and admire for his skill but at the same time feel a certain superiority to. Ted Williams, Joe DiMaggio, and Stan Musial were respected but never attained Berra's lovability quotient because they were above the masses—talented, good-looking, poised supermen.

Yogi the man is not a lovable teddy bear: He is slow to respond because he is relatively inarticulate, filled with the innate suspicion of the slum kid, prone to bits of sudden crudeness when he thinks he is being put on the spot or conned.

"How the * * * * should I know?" he will answer a harmless question from a stranger. With a man he trusts, he will sit down and explain his answers.

Yogi the myth is funny, egged into grammatical mistakes and non sequiturs by those who record the mouthings of the famous. But the man's words, separated from their delivery, usually make sense.

When he broke into the big leagues as a tangle-footed catcher, Bill Dickey was assigned to help him. "Dickey is learning me his experience," said Yogi.

Of a well-known restaurant: "Nobody goes there any more because it's too crowded."

Of the October shadows in Yankee Stadium's left field: "It gets late out there early."

Of seeing a performance of Tosca in Milan: "It was pretty good. Even the music was nice."

The lines are funny only coming from the myth. The man, of course, is making sense even if the words don't quite come out right,

Aug. 24, 1964: Casey Stengel, Mickey Mantle, and Yogi Berra share a laugh at Shea Stadium. (Larry C. Morris/The New York Times)

Berra has come far since his birth in St. Louis on May 12 1925. He was signed by the Yankee organization in 1942, and after a Navy hitch was brought up to the big club in 1946.

Married since 1949 to a beautiful blonde, with three sons—13, 11, and 6 years old—Berra is involved in many outside dealings. They include an executive position with the Yoo-Hoo Beverage Company, a chocolate soft-drink concern that didn't make money until Yogi was brought in.

Open Door for a Clown

He dresses like an executive now, plays golf, rarely reads comic books, and follows hockey, basketball, and football as an avid fan. He has continued to allow people to regard him as an amiable clown because it brings him quick acceptance, despite ample proof, on field and off, that he is intelligent, shrewd, and opportunistic.

But he is still a sensitive man perhaps bothered when people point him out as an example of "democracy at work," or as captain of the mythical "all-ugly baseball team."

He is still a man who could sit in the back of the Yankee plane several years ago reading a children's book of a zoo in which some wit had written a ballplayer's name under each animal.

He roared with laughter because Jim Coates was a raccoon, Bill Skowron a moose, and Marshall Bridges a fox. But his face turned red when he got to the last page, roaring "That's not funny," at the picture of a gorilla under which had been written, "Guess Who?" ∎

Yogi Berra reclines in the manager's office. (Ernie Sisto/The New York Times)

The Peerless Leader

By Arthur Daley • March 1, 1964

FORT LAUDERDALE, Fla., Feb. 29—Whitey Ford, the new pitching coach of the Yankees, was wearing a look of utter frustration when he rushed into the clubhouse just before a session of the preliminary rookie school a week or so ago. He hastened to his practically fearless leader, Yogi Berra, the new manager of the Bombers.

I'm embarrassed, Yog," said Whitey. "One of the kids said to me, 'Am I pitching today?' All I could do was mumble and tell him I'd let him know later on because I suddenly realized I couldn't remember who he was. Worse than that, he was sitting against the wall and I couldn't peek at the number on his back. Whatcha do in a case like that?"

"Do what I done the other day," said Yogi. "You get him on his feet and stall until you get a peek at his number. Then you compare it against the names on your list. That's what I done with Jim somebody.

Yogi has all the answers already.

A new air of authority has enveloped Lawrence Peter Berra and a new serenity, too. The strangest part of it all is that none of these characteristics seems awkwardly misplaced when superimposed on the image of the old Yogi Berra.

He's the same good-natured, friendly fellow he always has been but the burden of his responsibilities has forced to the surface qualities that had laid dormant. By golly, it's hard to believe but he even appears to have acquired a certain dignity and firmness.

He was able to be unconcerned the other day when the varsity battery men reported for their first workout and he will be the same when the rest of the squad checks in a few days hence. The toughest session for him was the opening of the rookie school a fortnight ago because this was his formal debut as a manager.

"I was too excited to sleep the night before,' he admitted, "I had butterflies in my stomach. It was just like the beginning of the World Series or the opening day of the season. You have the jitters until the first pitch is thrown. Then you just say to yourself, 'Here we go,' and you're all right. Like Ralph Houk says, 'The easiest part of this sport is when the game starts.'"

The rookie school had to bring back one vivid memory to Yogi because that's where it all began one year ago. He got to talking about it in fond recollection.

"I was at the rookie school last year because I was a coach," said Yogi, "and the very first day Ralph took me off to a corner.

"'How would you like to manage?' he said.

"'Manage who?' I said.

'Here. The Yankees.' he said.

"'Where the hell are you going?' I said.

"'I'm going to the front office as general manager,' he said. That afternoon I went with him and Roy Hamey to Dan Topping's yacht. We settled it then. Houk would succeed Hamey as general manager and I would succeed Houk as manager. But the deal was to be kept a secret until sometime after the World Series. My wife still can't believe I could keep a secret that long. To tell you the truth, I can't either. But I did."

Doubt as to Yogi's ability to handle his new role is fast disappearing. He is deporting himself as an executive as he deported himself at bat—with a graceful fluidity and natural ease. One early convert—presuming he even needed conversion—was Joe DiMaggio. Perhaps the Yankee Clipper helped because he was like all the other coaches at the first meeting the new commander in chief held with his staff. The Jolter was respectful and attentive, thereby giving Berra the huge morale boost he needed.

"Yogi is going to do all right," said DiMadge. "I learned long ago that no one should ever sell Yogi short. I still can remember the first time I ever noticed him. And you must admit he's a difficult man to avoid noticing. He had joined the team late in 1946 and I never was aware of him until I saw this peculiar looking creature waddling up to the plate with a bat in his hands for his, first swing at major league pitching.

Yogi Berra shaves as he listens to the radio for news of the pennant race. (AP Images)

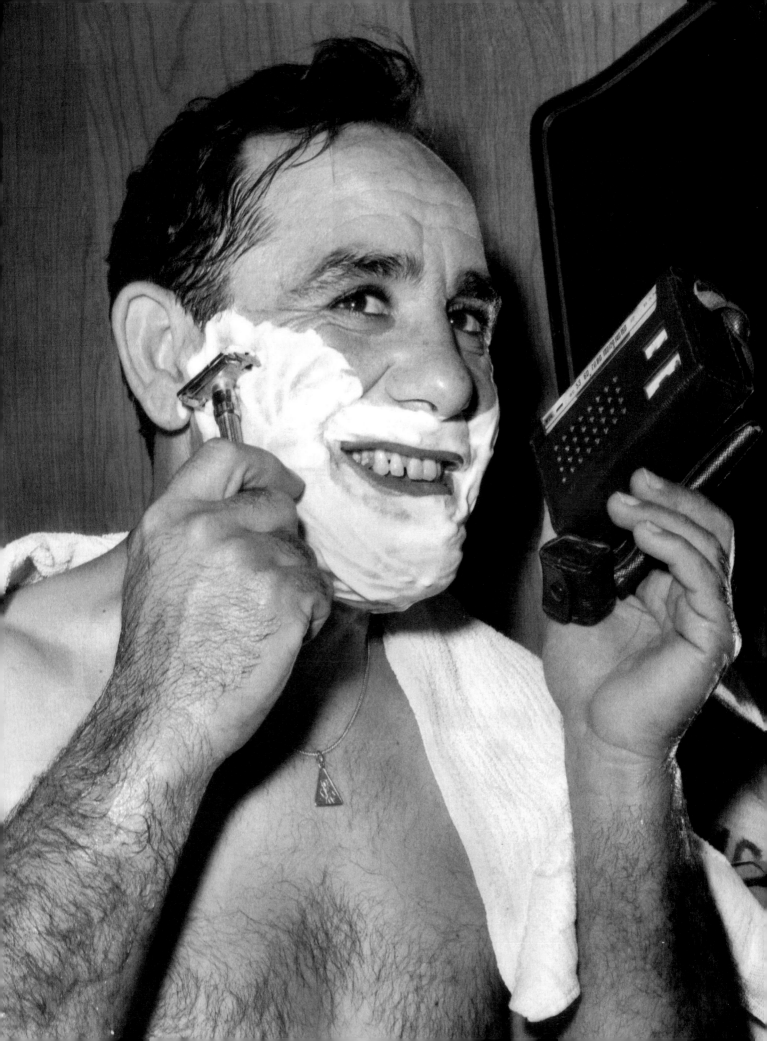

"One swing and—boffo! He'd hit the first pitch into the stands for a home run. That's when I began to pay attention to him and I've been paying attention ever since." Yogi gazed fondly on his old idol and puffed on a cigar somewhat distastefully.

"I gave up cigarettes for Lent," he said, "and I just smoke one or two of these damn things a day. I hate them but they ease that craving for the butts. Ha, ha, maybe they make me look more like a manager.

"The Yankees this year? I expect to win because I think we have the best team."

He's starting to talk with the brisk, unshakable confidence of a manager. More important, he acts like one, too. ■

Berra: A Losing Winner

By Leonard Koppett • October 17, 1964

Why was Yogi Berra discharged as manager of the Yankees, even though the team won the pennant?

He was dropped because most of his players felt he was not a good manager and because the front office agreed with them.

What was wrong with the way he managed?

He was not "smart," he was not good at "handling men," and his authority was often flouted. Those, at least, were the views among most of his critics, not all of whom were necessarily objective.

Actually, Yogi was true to himself and his abilities, and handled his managerial responsibilities in exactly the fashion that those who knew him expected. Whatever shortcomings he possessed, they were certainly well-known and predictable when Dan Topping and Ralph Houk decided to make him the manager.

When Yogi was announced as Houk's successor a year ago, it came as a shock to most of the players, who had all but worshiped Houk. The situation dated back to the closing years of Casey Stengel's regime.

The younger players of that time—among them Tony Kubek, Bobby Richardson, John Blanchard, Clete Boyer,

Joe DiMaggio and Yogi Berra share a moment at Yankees Rookie Camp in 1964. (Ernie Sisto/The New York Times)

Ralph Terry, and Roger Maris—never felt any particular affection for Stengel. He criticized them in public, he was sometimes abusive in private, he appeared to be too old to be alert and to be too severe.

When Houk became manager, it was like a release from reform school for most of the team. A fine practical psychologist, a born leader, an extremely intelligent and tough-minded man, Houk not only inspired confidence in his sound, orthodox baseball judgment, but also had the knack of "handling men."

When Houk suddenly took the opportunity to move up, most of the players felt abandoned. They didn't consider Yogi bright enough to manage; they hadn't particularly liked him as a teammate, because they found in him a tendency to second-guess others; and many of them resented Yogi's famous "image," which they felt was "created by the writers."

Before the 1964 season began, therefore, most of the players had prepared excuses for themselves, consciously or subconsciously, vocally or privately. Being good Yankees, none would talk about it out loud. The Yankee percentage of success in keeping secrets is considerably higher even than their impressive won-lost statistics.

Only late in the season did the sounds of despair rise to the surface.

"They took away from us the best manager in baseball," one of the articulate ones summed it up. "They took away the best pitching coach, Johnny Sain; the best batting coach, Wally Moses; they've weakened the bench because of the bonus rule. How do they expect us to win?"

With this attitude, Berra was on the spot. In retrospect, he couldn't win. Whatever went wrong would be his fault in the minds of the players. If a man didn't hustle, didn't stay in shape, didn't find his own way out of a slump, it was Berra's fault for not making him do it; if anything turned out right, the players believed, it was because they were good enough to overcome the handicaps put in their path.

This was almost exactly a repetition of the 1960 attitude toward Stengel.

And it was true that Berra did not possess Houk's unusual talents; the mystery was why anyone would expect him to.

Whatever anyone else did, Whitey Ford gave Berra 100 percent support this year. Mickey Mantle was completely cooperative. Most of the others, however, let their contempt show by degrees—and the front office couldn't avoid seeing that.

So, with talent as rich as the Yankee roster contains, Houk had to face up to the fact that his original move was wrong. What he expected is hard to fathom. The Yankees had been winning easily, and didn't like it because the gate lagged; they named Berra, used his "image," had the close race they yearned for, came out of it victorious—and drew still fewer people.

Now they'll go back to trying to win big with a "smart" manager. If he's smart, he'll concentrate on making the sensitive Yankees like him; but the effect on the sensitive public will remain uncertain. ∎

Yogi Berra hands his new contract to George Weiss, general manager of the club.
(Ernie Sisto/The New York Times)

4

Mets Coach and Manager

Berra Signs Two-Year Contract with Mets

By Leonard Koppett • November 18, 1964

With all the unexpectedness of the sun rising in the East, Yogi Berra appeared at Shea Stadium yesterday and officially began his New York Mets career after 18 years as a New York Yankee.

Berra, who was dismissed as the manager of the Yankees the day after they lost the World Series to the St. Louis Cardinals, will be a coach for the Mets under Casey Stengel. He also will be a pinch-hitter if he finds he can regain his batting eye during spring training.

He will collect $35,000 a year for two years from the Mets for serving as coach, whether or not he returns to the active list. He will also collect $25,000 from the Yankees, as a sort of parting gift or goodwill gesture.

Most likely, Berra will coach at first base, a function he performed for the Yankees during the 1963 season, when he was still active as a pinch-hitter and being groomed for the manager's job. With the Mets, Yogi isn't being groomed for anything, but speculation: that he will eventually succeed Stengel.

In explaining his decision, Berra stressed two things: his desire to remain "in uniform," and his lack of bitterness toward the Yankees.

"Right after the World Series, when I wasn't rehired, it was a blow," Yogi said. "But all clubs make changes, and they wanted to make a change, so I understood that. I came out with a good contract, so what was there to complain about? They (Ralph Houk and Dan Topping) brought up the point about me getting the $25,000 even if I left, and that sounded good.

"Then it was too early to think of changing. But after a while a lot of people told me, why don't you go with the Mets—writers and so forth—and so I called Casey in California. I had other offers, too—I won't mention the clubs—to be a coach and player, but I wanted to stay-in New York because I consider that my hometown now.

"First, though, I had to talk to Casey. I said, if Weiss asks me, do you want me, and he said yes."

George Weiss, the president of the Mets, broke in at that point.

"He talked to Casey before I talked to him," said Weiss. "Then he said he wanted to think about it, and finally he let me know on Friday that he had decided."

Berra was asked if he had notified the Yankees of his decision.

"Yes," he replied, "I sent Houk a wire."

Manager of the Mets, Yogi Berra, smiles for the camera. (Ernie Sisto/The New York Times)

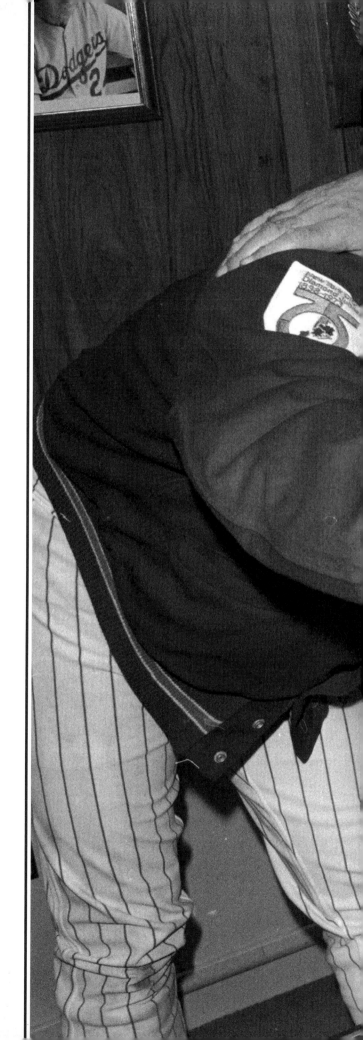

When?

"About an hour ago."

That reply brought an explosion of laughter, and Weiss stepped in to explain. "We only got together on final details this morning," he said.

More questions were asked about Berra's feelings toward the Yankees.

"No, I don't feel I was wronged," said Berra. "They hired me off the St. Louis sandlots when the Browns and Cardinals didn't want me, and I was happy there for 18 years. They never did me any wrong. But I'm also glad to be with an up-and-coming young club, like the Mets."

Later in the day, the Yankees issued a statement. It read:

"The Yankees wish Yogi Berra continued success in his new post with the New York Mets. Yogi has been one of the truly great Yankees and, while we were hoping he would continue in our organization, we can understand his desire to remain in uniform. We are proud to have had Yogi as a Yankee since 1946 and all of us join in wishing the Berras the best of luck in the future."

If he had stayed with the Yankees, Berra would have had a loosely defined job as "field consultant," scouting and doing special projects for Houk.

"The main thing," said Yogi, "was that I didn't feel I wanted to give up being in uniform, in contact with the ball players, and with you writers, instead of off in the stands at some other game. If I was 10 years older, it would be different, but I'm only 39. Besides, I can get in two more years on the pension plan and reach 20, which is the maximum.

"My wife, Carmen, and my boys felt the same way, that I belong down on the field. Right now I'm only going to be a coach, but if I do want to manage again, I'm under a good man in Casey, I learned a lot from him in 10 years, and I can learn a lot more." ■

Tom Seaver and Yogi Berra let the world know what they think of the 1973 Mets, who would go on to win the National League pennant. (Getty Images)

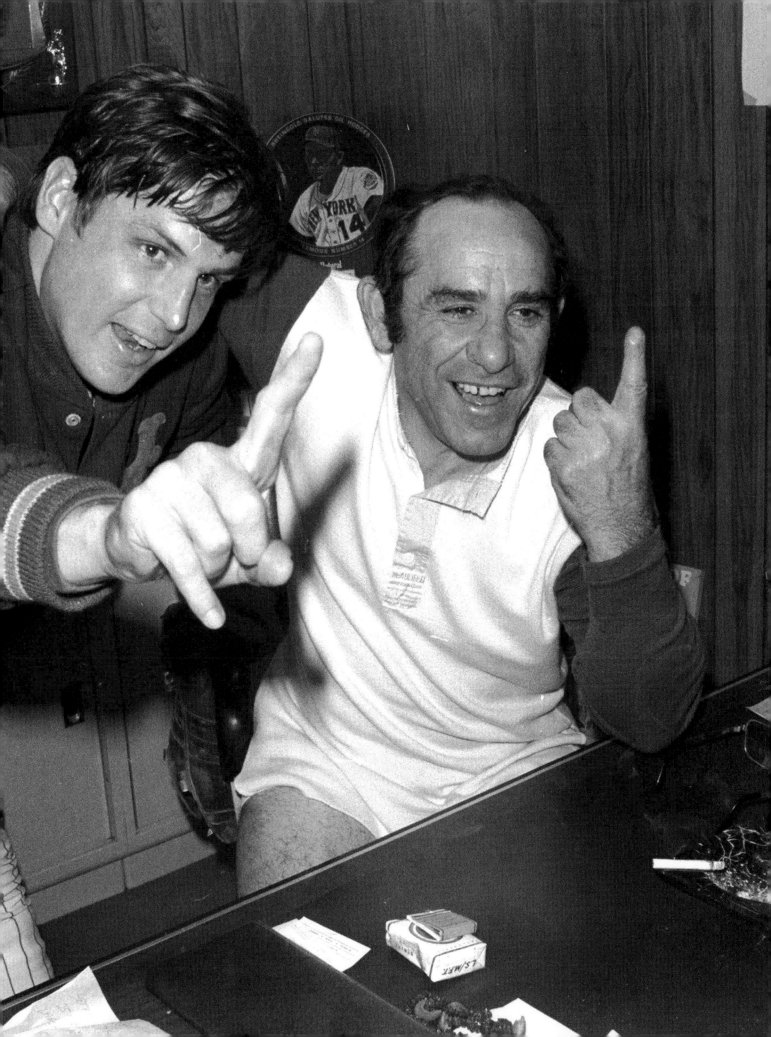

Mets Dismiss Berra and Name McMillan

By Joseph Durso • August 7, 1975

New York baseball was struck by its second blockbuster of the week yesterday when Yogi Berra was dismissed as manager of the Mets and replaced by one of his coaches, Roy McMillan.

The switch was announced in the same room in Shea Stadium where the Yankees made similar news five days earlier, dropping Bill Virdon as manager in favor of Billy Martin. At that time, the Mets were in Pittsburgh winning their third straight game over the first-place Pirates, but the next day they spiraled into a five-game losing streak that set the stage for Berra's exit.

For Berra, the one-time catcher who hit 358 home runs for the great Yankee teams a generation ago, the dismissal added more lore to his 30-year career as player, coach, manager, and folk-hero: He also was discharged by the Yankees in 1964 after one year as their manager, though they won the American League pennant and missed winning the World Series by one game.

The Mets said their decision had been considered at various times for the last year but had been finally reached during Tuesday night's double-header against the Montreal Expos, which the Mets lost without scoring a run. They hired McMillan at midnight as interim manager for the rest of the season and notified Berra by telephone yesterday morning at 9:15. And like Virdon of the Yankees, he still had one year left on his contract and will be paid for not managing through the 1976 season.

"It's a decision that has been going through our heads for some time," said M. Donald Grant, chairman of the Mets' board of directors, who promoted Berra to manager when Gil Hodges died of a heart attack in April 1972. "It had nothing to do with falling attendance, dissension on the team, the recent problem we had over Cleon Jones, or the Yankees' change of managers. Nothing had anything to do with it but the performance of the team and what happened Monday and Tuesday on the field climaxed our thinking." ∎

Yogi Berra poses in the office of his Montclair, N.J., home on Wednesday, August 7, 1975, after receiving word earlier in the day that he had been fired as manager of the Mets. On the firing, Berra commented, "It happens." (AP Photo)

Sports of the Times: Yogi Berra

By Red Smith • August 7, 1975

On his way to the Baseball Hall of Fame, Yogi Berra spent 17 summers observing the methods of managers named Bucky Harris, Casey Stengel, and Ralph Houk. "You can observe a lot by watching,' he said. Then he tried his hand and brain at the job, and steered the Yankees to a pennant in his first year. In that autumn of 1964 the Yankees lost the seventh game of the World Series to Bob Gibson and the St. Louis Cardinals. The next day Berra was out of a job. When Gil Hodges died suddenly just before the 1972 season, Yogi succeeded to command of the New York Mets. Halfway through his second summer, the team floundered badly, but rumors that Yogi might be fired were put half to rest by M. Donald Grant, chairman of the board. M. Donald said it wouldn't happen unless the fans insisted. So the Mets won their half of the pennant, whipped Cincinnati for the other half and went the limit of seven games against Oakland before losing the World Series. Grateful management gave Yogi a new contract running through 1976. Today he is unemployed again, but Grant did not blame his dismissal on pressure from the fans. "This is a matter that has been hanging over our heads for a long time," he said, whatever that meant.

Ralph Houk, who as general manager of the Yankees took responsibility for letting Yogi go in 1964, said at the time that it would have happened even if the team had won the World Series. Then four days later he hired Johnny Keane, the manager whose team had won the Series.

The Quiet Leader

There are two cardinal sins that get managers fired. One is losing ball games. The other is "losing control of the players." Houk indicated that it was the latter that cost Yogi his job with the Yankees. The circumstances suggest that M. Donald Grant feels the same way about this summer.

This brings up a question: Can a man lose something he never had? Yogi is a low-keyed leader. He has a naturally sweet disposition, seldom gets excited and rarely loses his temper. If he ever put his foot down with the Mets, he was careful to remove his spikes first. In fact, the incident that led up to his discharge by the Yankees may have been the only time he was known to flip his lid.

This was the mildly comic affair involving Phil Linz and his harmonica. The blithe Linz, then an infielder with the Yankees, committed the social error of striking up a tune on the team bus after a defeat. The manager told him to knock it off. Linz didn't hear him. In an uncharacteristic burst, Yogi swept the mouth organ aside.

It was a small ruckus that made big headlines. Curiously, the Yankees won from that day forward, beating the White Sox home by one game. Apparently, though, the front office was convinced that a man so deficient in musical appreciation would not do as manager.

That Jones Boy

Grant said yesterday that the recent trouble with Cleon Jones had nothing to do with Yogi's dismissal, but the parallel with the Linz case cannot be ignored. The difference is that it wasn't Yogi who lost his cool and precipitated the Jones rhubarb, it was M. Donald Grant.

After a charge of indecent exposure against Jones was dropped in St. Petersburg, Florida, last spring, it

Mets manager Yogi Berra waves to the fans. (Robert Walker/The New York Times)

was Grant who dragged Cleon and his wife before the New York press and extracted a public apology. With that exercise in medieval torture, communication between Jones and the ball club broke down. Understandably.

It was the absence of communication that caused the recent dust-up when Jones, having gone into a game as pinch-batter, defied Yogi's order to stay in as the left fielder. Once that happened, the reason why it had happened became secondary to Yogi, If he let the rebel get away with rebellion, he was finished as manager. He was right to insist on a showdown, but it was too late.

Jones did get away with his rebellion. He got his unconditional release and the right to sell his services to the highest bidder, And Yogi, it turned out, was finished. Somebody had to be the fall guy. Chairmen of the board hardly ever are.

Naming Roy McMillan interim manager was all right, but it's too bad the Mets didn't have the wit to hire Bill Virdon. The Yankees have been dickering with Cleon Jones. It would have been poetic justice for the Mets to grab the Yankees' deposed manager. They didn't, though. They didn't have the corpus delicti at Yogi's wake, either. He was said to be playing golf in New Jersey. I hope he hit them straight and putted like an angel. ■

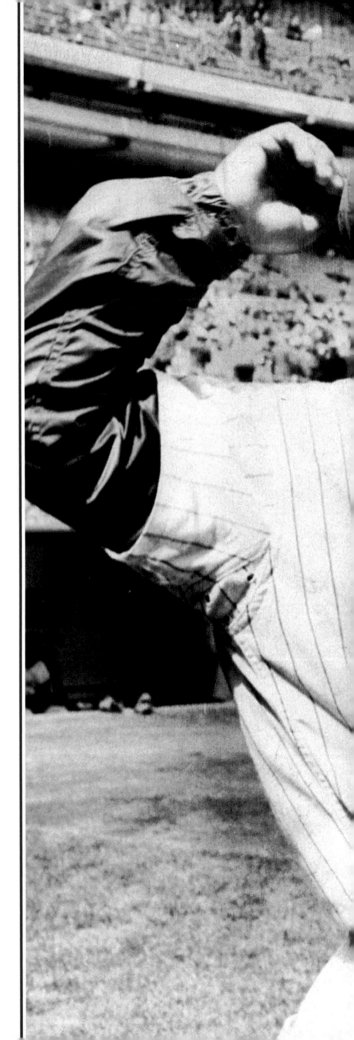

New York Mets' coach Yogi Berra (left) and San Francisco Giants' great Willie Mays talk before the start of a game at Shea Stadium. (Getty Images)

5

Yankees Manager 1984-1985

Yogi's Back in Style

By George Vecsey • December 17, 1983

Yogi Berra's second regime as Yankee manager began yesterday with the contented air of a man settling into his favorite easy chair. Yogi said he would welcome advice from his coaches because "four heads are better than one" and he teased his friends in the press that "you guys ain't gonna get too much from me."

As soon as he could, he slipped away from the microphones and mingled with the baseball people in the crush. He lighted a cigarette, shifted his weight from one foot to the other and made small talk, sotto voce, in his familiar guttural voice.

The three Yankee players attending Yogi's coronation—Willie Randolph, Steve Kemp and Rick Cerone—noted that Yogi had been able to slip into casual conversation while he was one of the cast of thousands of Yankee coaches. And they predicted he would be the same way when the Yankees start work in February.

"People change—but I don't think Yogi will," Randolph said. "You can talk to him."

Randolph meant baseball talk, the little nuts-and-bolts shop talk that people need in any business. He

meant that Berra had always been there, shuffling unobtrusively around the clubhouse, listening and offering advice that did not make headlines, did not make waves, but that helped people do their jobs a little better.

Whether this will translate into a long reign as Yankee manager is another question. Billy Martin raised the Yankee record by 12 games and the Yankee attendance by 300,000 in 1983 and still George Steinbrenner scuttled him yesterday. Of course, Steinbrenner does not like the word "fired."

Steinbrenner said: "You can chose to look at it that way, but I'm shifting personnel. Nobody's been fired." George Steinbrenner does not fire managers: He merely shifts them. Berra's appointment is the 11th "shift" in Steinbrenner's first decade. Berra knows the odds, and he can even laugh at the inevitable conflicts weeks or months before they happen: "So what? That don't bother me. I don't care what he does."

Berra has observed most of Steinbrenner's changes up close since coming back from the Mets in 1976. He brought his fabled good luck back with him (nothing is more secure about flying through a thunderstorm than having Yogi Berra in the same plane) and the Yankees won their first pennant since 1964, when the manager was one Lawrence Peter Berra.

Yogi Berra directs his players from the bench in the 1984 season opener in Kansas City. (AP Images)

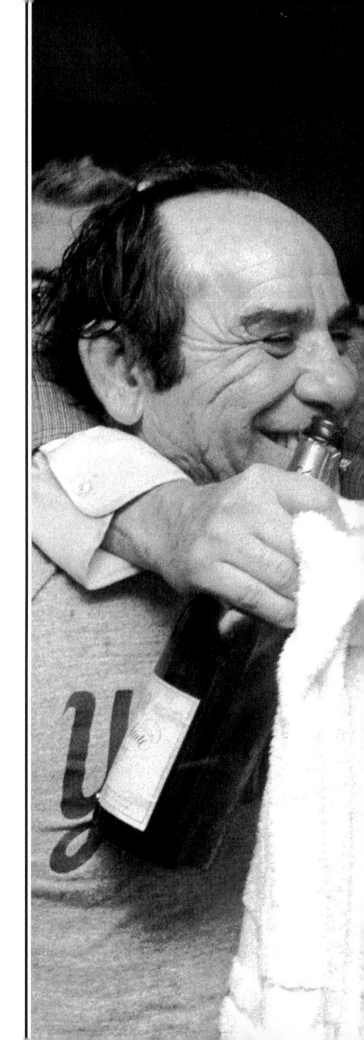

In his eight years back as Yankee coach, Berra has been in the dugout for the feuds, the threats, the comings and the goings, the glories and the tragedies. He has kept his head while others were losing theirs. He has turned down the Yankee managing job at least twice during midseason crises because "I like to start a season; your mind can be more open."

It is just an extension of the Berra fortune that he waited long enough until his homey professionalism became a priority for the start of the season, worth a two-year contract. And he was able to joke, "I hope he takes good care of me, too," a reference to the lucrative "shift" for Billy Martin.

There was far more curiosity about Steinbrenner's thinking and Martin's health than there was about Yogi. Yogi is old stuff, like the favorite easy chair or the broken-in slippers waiting alongside it.

The baseball people in the crowd had good things to say about Berra. They said he never stopped thinking and working and caring.

Gene Michael, who will move from being a scout to third-base coach, was the manager in two different "shifts." Michael says he relied on Berra, the once and future manager.

"Yogi would come over to me and say, 'Maybe you should rest Nettles against this left-hander,' or he'd say, 'Boston hasn't seen many right-handers lately, maybe we should use two against them in the next series.'"

Not all coaches are secure enough to offer flat-out advice like this, but Yogi Berra is one of a kind, a national institution. Martin, who ignored and even humiliated some of his coaches, would listen to Berra. The players knew this. It was their best shot at getting through to the increasingly moody and distant manager.

This is the same Yogi Berra who could not coax winning attitudes from some of the Mets before, during, and after his 1973 pennant. He is the same man who slapped the harmonica from the hands of Phil Linz in the back of a bus just before the Yankees made their pennant run in 1964.

George Steinbrenner hugs coach Yogi Berra (left) and manager Billy Martin as they celebrate victory with champagne. (Getty Images)

"I don't get mad very often," Berra said yesterday, agreeing that the harmonica incident "was one of those times."

There have been times when Berra seemed light years removed from the new breed of players who demanded "communication," and with the new breed of journalists who wanted some depth in their answers. That won't change, even though Berra said yesterday: "I feel I understand the ballplayers of today."

Maybe he does; maybe he doesn't. Nobody is hiring him for his value as a glib motivator of young millionaires. He is Yogi Berra, the man who knows all the secrets of the clubhouse, the man the players trusted during the turmoil, the former manager whose mind never stopped churning with baseball details. He has won a pennant for both teams he has managed, and with Berra-style patience he waited for his time to come around again. ■

Yogi's History Lesson

By Jane Gross • March 25, 1984

FORT LAUDERDALE, Fla., March 24—It is not just an ordinary day at the ball park when the British Broadcasting Company interviews Yogi Berra, or at least tries to.

The BBC announcer, his syllables clipped and his tone haughty, was looking for a baseball history lesson. "When did the game begin?" he asked the Yankee manager, who shrugged, mumbled, and turned for help to Bill Bergesch.

The team's vice president, whose answer to most questions is "no comment," shrugged and mumbled himself, as helpless as Berra. The camera kept whirring and the microphone was poised near Berra's mouth. After a long pause Berra rose to the occasion.

"Eighteen something, wasn't it?" Berra finally replied. ■

Yankees manager Yogi Berra gesturing during a game. (Mike Maple/The New York Times)

On Pinch-Hitting for Your Son

By Dave Anderson • April 21, 1985

With two hits in his three times at bat last Friday night, Dale Berra had lifted his average to .348, but now, with the Yankees losing, 2–1, to the Cleveland Indians, he trotted in from third base for the bottom of the ninth inning. Dale Berra was scheduled to be the Yankees' second batter, but he realized that the manager might have something else in mind.

"Dad," he said to Yogi Berra, "you gonna hit for me?"

"If Billy Sample don't get on, yeah," his father said.

Billy Sample lifted a fly ball to center field. In the on-deck circle, Dale Berra stopped swinging his bats, turned and walked into the dugout from which Ron Hassey, a left-handed batter, emerged as a pinch-hitter. And if Connie Mack never used a pinch-hitter for his son Earle, who had only 16 times at bat for the Philadelphia A's back in 1910, 1911, and 1914, then Friday night's move was a small but significant moment in major-league history—the first time a manager sat down his son for a pinch-hitter.

But in another sense, it was also the first time that a son anticipated being sat down by his father for a pinch-hitter.

"No big deal," Dale Berra was saying now in the Yankee clubhouse. "If Sample gets on, I stay in and bunt him over. If he gets a double, I might swing away. But he didn't get on and we needed the long ball against a right-hand pitcher. No big deal."

With a .238 career batting average for the Pittsburgh Pirates before joining the Yankees this season, Dale Berra has not been immune to being replaced by a pinch-hitter.

"I once got pinch-hit for by Chuck Tanner when I was 3 for 3," he said of the Pirates' manager. "Hey, that's baseball, that's what pinch-hitters are for.

Casey Stengel, manager of the New York Mets, and Yogi Berra, manager of the New York Yankees, at Shea Stadium. (Larry C. Morris/The New York Times)

Friday night the Berras drove to the Stadium in separate cars from their nearby homes in New Jersey, but for yesterday's game they rode together.

"Day games, we'll probably come in together a lot," Yogi Berra said. "I always get to the ball park early, so if we come over together for day games, it makes him go to bed early."

After his son's errors Tuesday and Thursday, the manager called him aside.

"I just told him, 'Take it easy, do what you're supposed to do,' " Yogi Berra said. "This is his first time here. He's happy to be here. He'll help." ∎

Berra Dismissed by Steinbrenner

By Michael Martinez • April 29, 1985

CHICAGO, April 28—George Steinbrenner, who said two months ago that Yogi Berra would be the Yankees' manager for the entire 1985 season no matter what, dismissed Berra today, just 16 games into the season, and brought back Billy Martin for his fourth term.

The appointment of Martin marks the 12th managerial change since Steinbrenner led a group that purchased the Yankees from CBS in 1973.

The task of informing Berra of his dismissal was given to Clyde King, the Yankee general manager, who spoke with Steinbrenner by telephone during the Yankees' game with the Chicago White Sox. According to King, Steinbrenner had decided to dismiss Berra even before the 4–3 Yankee defeat, the team's third straight loss.

King notified Berra of his dismissal shortly after the game. Steinbrenner also telephoned Berra an hour later in the visiting clubhouse at Comiskey Park.

"Today's game had no bearing on what happened," King said afterward. "Mr. Steinbrenner said he hoped to see Yogi go out a winner. Mr. Steinbrenner said he didn't sleep last night. He said he agonized all night over this."

Yogi Berra with George Steinbrenner at a Yankees news conference on Dec. 16, 1984. (AP Images)

Steinbrenner issued a statement through the Yankee publicity department, announcing the dismissal. Steinbrenner was quoted as saying, "This action has been taken by the Yankees, and we feel that it is in the best interests of the club." It also said that Steinbrenner told King "he would rather fire 25 players than to fire Yogi, but we all know that would be impossible."

Berra, who remained behind closed doors for nearly a half hour after receiving the news, smiled when reporters finally entered the small office. His son, Dale, had already spent several minutes with his father and emerged with tears in his eyes.

"I'm in a very good mood," Yogi Berra said. "This is still a very good ball club, and they're getting a good manager in Billy Martin. I don't think my players laid down on me."

Berra refused to criticize Steinbrenner for his decision to release the manager. "He's the boss," Berra said. "He can do what he wants. I'm used to this. This is the third time I've been fired. That's what this game is—managers are hired to be fired. I know it's an old saying, but that's what it is."

Berra had been dismissed twice before, once by the Mets, whom he managed from 1972 to 1975, taking them to the World Series in 1973, and by the Yankees, whom he managed to a pennant in 1964 but lost in the World Series.

Asked if he would accept another position with the club, Berra said: "I don't know. He hasn't asked me yet. My contract says I don't have to do anything. Right now, I'm just gonna go home and play golf."

Berra said he felt no relief that the turmoil of the last three weeks, which included continual criticisms from Steinbrenner over the team's play and what he termed "lack of discipline," was over.

Berra shook his head. "I'd still like to stay here," he said. "But like I said, he's the boss."

At the same time, Berra intimated that the team had yet to play at its full capacity. "We had injuries at the beginning of the season," he said. "We've got two or three guys who are still in spring training."

Did he feel he was treated fairly by Steinbrenner?

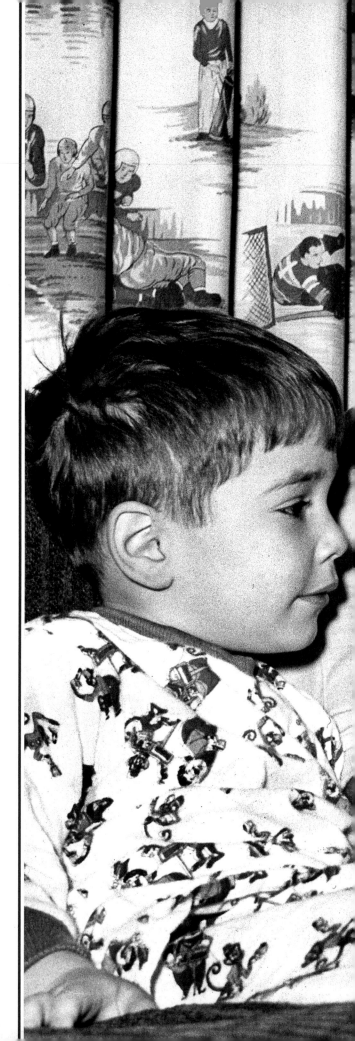

Yogi Berra reads to his grandson. (Getty Images)

"I don't know if I did or not," he answered. "But I still think this club is gonna turn itself around."

Few players were willing to discuss Berra's sudden dismissal. Several, including Dave Winfield, Willie Randolph, and Don Baylor, three of the most outspoken members of the team, refused to comment. But Baylor, after reading the prepared statement that had been handed out to reporters, kicked over a trashcan in the clubhouse.

The team left after the game for Texas, but Berra was not on board the charter flight. He walked through the clubhouse, saying goodbye to players and wishing them well, then stopped at his son's locker. "Are you going home?" Dale asked. "Yeah," said Yogi. "Home." ∎

When Yogi Threw His Cigarettes

By Dave Anderson • March 28, 1989

In bookstores all over the country, this year's baseball books are on display. And of all the glossy dust jackets, the most appealing shows Yogi Berra, wearing glasses and a gray Yankee road uniform, sitting in a dugout with his left hand atop his Yankee cap as if he were deciding whether or not to tell why George Steinbrenner dismissed him as manager only 16 games into the 1985 season.

This is Yogi Berra's autobiography: Yogi: It Ain't Over (McGraw-Hill).

And for anyone who still wonders about Yogi's sudden discharge, it ain't a secret anymore. At first his explanation sounds like a typical Yogi non sequitur: a pack of cigarettes. But he didn't smoke them, he threw them. And it wasn't in 1985, it was the year before. But let the current Houston Astros' coach tell it the way he told Tom Horton, his collaborator.

"I don't get mad easy and even when I do I don't stay mad. I got mad in 1984. We had a meeting in the owner's office. We had too many meetings, I thought.

Manager Yogi Berra argues with the umpire for the second time on June 6, 1984, as he goes to the mound to yank pitcher Jose Rijo. Berra's outburst gets him an early exit from the game. (AP Images)

"The 24 guys I wanted to be on the team were not the same guys who the owner wanted on the team. It wasn't just one guy.... It was four or five guys who the owner wanted and the coaches and I didn't.... We talked a lot and I said something like, 'If you want that team, can I say that this is your team if we lose?'... I knew that the coaches and I knew more about judging baseball ability than anyone else in the room.

"Anyway, this meeting got so bad that I called the owner some bad names and threw a pack of cigarettes at him.

One of the coaches said I threw the pack down on his desk and it bounced up and hit him. I don't know. I know I threw them, and I know I was hot.

"He said, 'Nobody ever talks to me that way,' or maybe it was 'Nobody can ever talk to me that way.' I have forgotten because when you get mad you do forget...

"He was mad, I was mad.... I wondered if the thrown pack of cigarettes came back my way the next year. What I mean is, the next year, 1985, I managed 16 games and it was over. I was never told why I was fired."

Yogi is also chronicled in the best of this year's baseball books, Summer of '49 (Morrow), David Halberstam's recreation of the season when the Yankees won the American League pennant by overtaking the Boston Red Sox with a two-game sweep at Yankee Stadium on the final weekend. Joe DiMaggio and Ted Williams dominate Halberstam's plot, but Yogi is identified as a pioneer of sorts.

Shortly after Frank Scott was fired as the Yankees' traveling secretary in 1950, he was in Yogi's home when he asked what time it was. Yogi opened a drawer and tossed him a watch. "Where did this come from?" Scott asked. Yogi opened the drawer again. In it were about 30 watches.

"That's what they give me when I make speeches."

Scott suggested that he represent Yogi in negotiating speaking engagements. That's how Yogi Berra emerged as the first member of those Yankee teams to have an agent. Now he's also got a publisher. ■

Hank Bauer and Yogi Berra in the Yankee Stadium locker room. (Ernie Sisto/The New York Times)

6

Astros Coach

A Happy Return

By Ira Berkow • March 24, 1986

KISSIMMEE, Fla.—In a period spanning a little more than 40 years, Yogi Berra has survived both D-Day and George Steinbrenner, and is alive and well and coaching in Kissimmee.

Lawrence Peter (Yogi) Berra is 60 years old and a long way from when he was 19 on June 6, 1944, and serving on a Navy landing craft at Normandy—"They called it the suicide squad," he said with a smile. And he is a long way from April 30, 1985, when, just 16 games into the season, Steinbrenner, the Yankees' principal owner and noted manager-dumper, dropped Berra as manager.

Berra rarely complains or backbites. All he said about his Steinbrenner past is, "I didn't get a fair shake."

Now, for the first time in his 40-year big-league baseball career, Berra wears neither the vertical blue pin-stripes of the Yankees nor the Mets but the horizontal orange of the Houston Astros, who are limbering up for the season in this tourist haven that is close by Disney World.

"I'm happy to be in a baseball uniform," Berra said. "The only difference now is the stripes are goin' the other way." He seems relaxed and content as he enters the ball field on a recent warm, sunny afternoon before a spring training game.

"Hi, Yogi," calls an opposing player for that afternoon's game, Bert Blyleven of the Twins, "How's Dale doin'?" "OK," said Berra, "OK." Berra walked past, and said to a companion, "That's one of the old Pirate guys."

Dale, of course, is Berra's son, an infielder for the Yankees, and a former teammate of Blyleven's when both were with the Pirates. Dale was traded to the Yankees and it seemed like the summer of 1985 was going to be an ideal one for the Berras. Yogi would be managing his son, a kind of dream come true; he was the first manager to have his son playing for him since Connie Mack and Earle Mack in the second decade of this century.

But the summer turned out to be one of the most trying in the lives of the Berras. Yogi was dismissed and Dale emerged as one of the major league players who gave testimony under immunity in last summer's headlined drug-related trials in Pittsburgh. Dale admitted to using cocaine. Shortly before a story about the use of cocaine by players, including Dale Berra, was about to be broken, a reporter went to Dale in the Yankee clubhouse and told Dale that the story was going to have to run.

Dale seemed stunned by the information that was uncovered and, knowing that there was nothing he could do to keep it from becoming public, said to the reporter, softly, "Does my father know?"

When this scenario was mentioned to Yogi Berra, sitting now on the Astros bench, he lowered his head and nodded. Someone close to the Berra family had

No more Pinstripes: Yogi Berra as a Houston Astros coach on March 6, 1987. (AP Images)

said that Yogi and Carmen "went through a lot of pa-
rental anguish" over the drug usage by Dale.

"I didn't understand why he did it," Berra said. "I
guess, you know, you go to parties and everyone's having a good time. But you gotta be able to say no. I said
that if he wants to stay in the game he'd have to kick
it. I hear it's like alcohol. You just gotta be able to stay
away from it. Dale's brothers got on him, too." Berra
has two other sons, Larry Jr. and Tim.

"I think he's all right now," Berra said. "It's hard
to follow how he does in the papers because they don't
run box scores down here. But I know he hit a home
run the other day. I gotta call him tonight. We talk on
the phone about every 10 days."

Now Berra rose to hit some fungoes to the outfielders. As he came out of the dugout, a woman nearby
requested his autograph. She handed him a scorecard
and a fountain pen. He held them close to his dark blue
Astro uniform top as he signed. When finished he noticed that his hands were now stained.

"Your pen kinda leaks," he said to the woman, his
eyebrows furrowed. Then Berra turned to a companion
and smiled. "Would you believe I got a white shirt on?
" he said. ■

Yogi Berra looks over the field with son Dale, a
shortstop with the Astros, before a game against
the Atlanta Braves on Aug. 15, 1987. (AP Images)

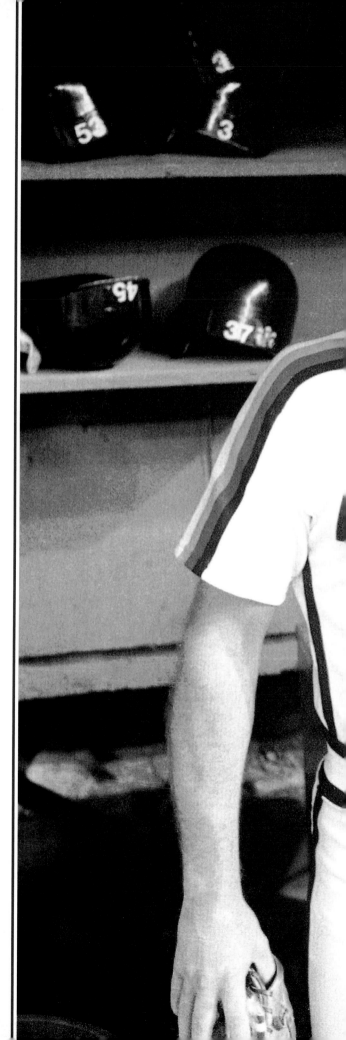

7

A Self-Imposed Exile

Berra Will Still Watch the Yanks from Afar

By Claire Smith • August 28, 1990

George Steinbrenner signed his resignation a week ago yesterday and tendered it the next day, leaving Yankee Stadium in other hands for the first time since 1972.

Is the Steinbrenner reign really over, though? Yogi Berra, an expert of sorts when it comes to gauging when things in baseball are, indeed, over, is not yet convinced. And that's important because Berra, who voluntarily became the Yankees' prodigal son, vowing not to return to Yankee Stadium until Steinbrenner packed and left for good, is not about to come back yet.

"To me, I don't think he's out of it yet, so I don't know when I'll come back," Berra said last week by telephone from his home in Montclair, New Jersey.

It's not that Berra wouldn't like to return. The Hall of Famer and arguably the greatest catcher ever misses the team that employed him as a player from 1946 through 1963, as a manager in 1964 and again in 1984–85, and as coach from 1976 through 1983. So Berra tracks the Yankees and the Mets, a team for which he briefly played as well as managed and coached.

"They got a pretty good-looking kid in Maas," said Berra, who watches the Yankees as well as the Mets on television. "A lot of those kids don't look bad. If they keep playing like that, I think they could be pretty good."

As for familiar faces, there aren't that many left to identify. "I think there's only the two I managed, Don Mattingly and Dave Righetti," Berra said. "I'd like to see them. And I know Stump. I like him. He was my coach, you know. But he got fired."

Reminded that Stump Merrill, the Yankees' manager, just got a two-year contract extension, Berra said; "I'm happy for him. But, you know, it don't mean a thing there. We'll see, I guess."

To talk to Berra is to listen to a man more stubborn than bitter, however. And to listen to a man with a long memory. He lived through a season in which he, too, supposedly enjoyed a vote of confidence.

In 1985, Steinbrenner said Berra was his manager for the year. Berra was dismissed after 16 games. It was then that Berra told his stunned players, including his son, Dale, to play hard for Billy Martin. It was then that Berra, after receiving an emotional ovation from the team as he was dropped off at O'Hare International in Chicago, walked away and never looked back.

He and Steinbrenner haven't exchanged a word since. "I waved at him in a winter meeting, once," Berra said. "But speak? Nope."

The Yankees are now playing the Yogi Berra video on their giant screen at the Stadium these days as part of their salute to great Yankee players. The last time the Berra video was shown was in April 1985.

Berra, who went on to serve as a coach for the Houston Astros until his retirement last year, has received an occasional invitation to Yankee old-timers games. He even was asked to attend a ceremony in his honor as the

Yogi Berra in front of his home in Montclair, N.J. (Larry Morris/The New York Times)

Yankees did something many agreed was long overdue: put up a plaque with Berra's likeness where the rest of the monuments to Yankee greats stand behind the left-field wall.

Berra did not attend any of those events, nor did he allow his family to do so. He also declined to attend a ceremony honoring Phil Rizzuto at this year's Old-Timers Day. Berra's reasons were well known and accepted by Rizzuto, his friend and former teammate.

Berra said he really doesn't spend much time thinking about Steinbrenner in this summer of the owner's discontent. He has been too busy attending charity golf tournaments, running the family racquetball club, spending time with his seven grandchildren and occasionally serving as adviser and scout for John McMullen, a friend and the owner of the Astros.

"This summer's been super," Berra said. "We have a lot of barbecues, believe me. And Carmen hasn't thrown me out of the house, yet. So, it's been all right."

One baseball event Berra refused to give up was the Hall of Fame ceremonies. He was one of a record 34 Hall of Famers in attendance this year as Joe Morgan and Jim Palmer were inducted. "To see Ted Williams and Al Lopez again, that was great," Berra said.

As for Steinbrenner, ordered by Commissioner Fay Vincent to relinquish operational control of the Yankees for having consorted with gambler, Howard Spira, does Berra feel for a man who had to give up his team because he finally conceded that some of his actions were not in the best interest of baseball?

Berra paused a moment, then said: "I can't tell about George, yet. You can never tell about George." ■

Members of the 1969 Mets—Yogi Berra, Nolan Ryan, Jerry Grote, Tom Seaver, and Jerry Koosman—at a pregame ceremony on Aug. 22, 2009. (AP Images)

An Ace for Berra

August 12, 1998

It wasn't over until the ball rolled in the hole, but when it did, at the Montclair Golf Club yesterday, Yogi Berra had made a hole-in-one.

The shot came during the Yogi Berra Celebrity Golf Classic, held annually to benefit the Boy Scouts of America. The former Yankee catcher, who plays right-handed but putts left-handed, did not need to putt at all as he stroked a perfect 4-iron 160 yards to the eight green on the first of the Montclair club's four nines. It was the first hole-in-one in Berra's lesser-known career as a golfer.

Berra's hole-in-one, however, is not considered official because it did not occur during an 18-hole round. As the tournament host, he hit a ball on that hole with every group. ■

It's Time for Yogi to Get Over It

By Harvey Araton • July 25, 1998

The town of Montclair, New Jersey, will have its second Hall of Fame baseball player tomorrow when Larry Doby is inducted in Cooperstown, New York. Not coincidentally, his neighbor in the leafy suburb happens to be on the Veterans Committee that voted him in more than a half-century after he integrated the American League.

Doby, in fact, ran into Yogi Berra recently and asked him if he was nervous back in 1972 when Berra made his own induction speech. Not really, Berra said. It is doubtful Doby will be either, given the odds and insensitivity he has stared down for much of his 73 years.

As the folksy master of the faux pas, Berra has himself become a national symbol of sporting valor for

Yogi Berra and George Steinbrenner saying goodbye after Berra forgave him, ending their 14-year feud. "Fourteen years, I'd say, is long enough," Berra said. (AP Images)

his refusal to set foot in Yankee Stadium for as long as George Steinbrenner remains the Yankees' owner. Recently, Sports Illustrated even asked Berra to pose for a cover story on the most principled people in sports. Berra, to his credit, said no.

He has never made his personal stand a public crusade, the way others have for him, usually around Old-Timers' Day, which is at Yankee Stadium today. When Steinbrenner fired Berra as manager after a handful of games in 1985, Berra said that's it, he was going home to Montclair and wouldn't be back. That is his choice, which he is certainly entitled to, but the reality is that he is not hurting Steinbrenner, only depriving nostalgic fans the privilege of seeing No. 8 once more inside the grand ballpark. He is unwittingly sending the wrong subliminal message that Steinbrenner, above all, is the Yankees.

Berra should get over the firing, and next year walk back into a stadium that is owned in part by tax-paying Yankee fans, not the man who holds its sweetheart lease. Go home again. Stand alongside Joe DiMaggio and Whitey Ford and Willie Randolph and, yes, Jim Bouton, all of whom were the Yankees, the way Paul O'Neill, Derek Jeter, and David Cone are now.

Yankee Stadium was Berra's house long before Steinbrenner knew his way out of Ohio. Berra should at least once in his remaining years experience the cheers, the looking up at the owner's box to let Steinbrenner know that banishing the manager from the dugout does not chase true greatness from the field.

They are not close friends, but Doby, for one, could tell Berra about the emotional rewards of holding his ground, of standing tall. When he was a young boy in Camden, South Carolina, rich white Northerners would stable their horses there during the winter. Once or twice a year, they would ride in or out of town, tossing pennies into the street for poor black children

From left to right: Stan Musial, Yogi Berra, and Ralph Kiner get together in 1975, just after Kiner was inducted into the Baseball Hall of Fame. (AP Images)

to chase. Doby has said that while he often watched this procession, he never once moved a muscle to pick up a coin.

He learned early not to jump at the bait, and when he joined the Cleveland Indians in July, 1947, he ignored the foul taunts, just as Jackie Robinson did in Brooklyn, beginning three months earlier. Doby played 13 years in the major leagues, won two home-run titles, was a seven-time All-Star, yet for 50 years, couldn't shake Robinson's shadow. The racist, ignorant and indifferent never defeated him, though. Never made him acquiesce, or run.

There is power in his presence, Doby apparently understands. He goes to Cooperstown today knowing that he never sold himself out for pennies and always waited patiently to make a real score. You can't change history, can't undo the bad that's already been done, but there is no significant achievement in just going away. Nothing gained, Yogi, by giving up the time and place that is rightfully yours. ∎

Yogi and the Boss Complete Makeup Game

By Harvey Araton • January 6, 1999

LITTLE FALLS, N.J., Jan. 5—Let the record show that a celebrated grudge held for nearly 14 years was dropped here a few minutes after 5 this evening when a contrite George Steinbrenner arrived at Yogi Berra's doorstep and thanked the self-exiled Yankee great for the opportunity to make this day necessary.

The Yankees' principal owner traveled from his home in Tampa, Florida, to the museum named for Berra on the campus of Montclair State University to apolo-

Yogi Berra, sitting beside his wife, Carmen, comments on the passing of Yankees owner George Steinbrenner on Tuesday, July 13, 2010. (AP Images)

gize, finally, for how he fired Berra as the team's manager 16 games into the 1985 season. The news of Berra's dismissal was delivered by Clyde King, another member of Steinbrenner's organization, and Berra vowed after that never to again set foot in Yankee Stadium as long as Steinbrenner owned the team.

This evening, Steinbrenner walked up to the front entrance of the museum, where Berra awaited him with his hand outstretched.

"Hello, Yogi," Steinbrenner said, cautiously.

"You're 10 minutes late," Berra quipped.

The man known as the Boss and the Hall of Fame catcher then ducked into a small office, accompanied by Berra's wife, Carmen. According to Mrs. Berra, Steinbrenner took Berra's hand, looked him in the eye and said: "I know I made a mistake by not letting you go personally. It's the worst mistake I ever made in baseball."

Berra replied, "I made a lot of mistakes in baseball, too." Then he gave Steinbrenner a tour of his museum, which formally opened last month, and coyly said he would strongly consider returning to the Stadium sometime next season, possibly on opening day or Old-Timers' Day, which is later in the summer. "I told him what he needed to do," Berra said. "He apologized. We'll see."

"If I could get Yogi to come back," said Steinbrenner, warming to the occasion, "I'd bring him over with a rickshaw across the George Washington Bridge."

Carmen Berra said she believed Steinbrenner's visit had nothing to do with business and everything to do with a clear conscience. "With the year 2000 coming, everyone is thinking about the future, about peace, about making things right," she said.

Along those lines, Steinbrenner admitted that the death of Mickey Mantle in 1996 and the near loss of Joe DiMaggio last month made him feel a sense of urgency in making amends. "There was a missing piece," he said, alluding to the recent record-setting, 125-victory Yankees season, and it was Berra. "He's got to forgive me and come back," he told Carmen Berra in a private

The Berras watching their son Dale play. (Carl T. Gossett/The New York Times)

moment, perhaps with the thought that Berra return to help raise the team's championship banner on opening day next spring, and make 1998 complete.

Berra, surprisingly, seemed to enjoy the public nature of the event, often tweaking Steinbrenner. He praised the Yankees' current managerial staff and told Steinbrenner not to interfere or he wouldn't show up for another 14 years. But mostly, he enjoyed being host to Steinbrenner, ushering him around the museum. "He's very proud of this," Carmen Berra said.

Though this was the house that Berra built and he, at 74, is six years older than Steinbrenner, he seemed like the wandering son returning to a paternal embrace when the two men hugged at the door, and said good-bye.

Steinbrenner, clutching a copy of Berra's latest book of original "Yogisms" and a Berra Museum shirt, said, "I'll talk to you soon."

The door closed. Berra, who coined the expression "It's not over till it's over," turned back.

"Fourteen years," he said, smiling. "It's over." ∎

Yogi Berra with his wife, Carmen, and his son Tim. (William Sauro/The New York Times)

8

The Legend

Legend Dons Cap at Legends Field

By Jack Curry • March 2, 1999

TAMPA, Fla., March 1—Yogi Berra visited Legends Field today and the first thing Joe Torre did was place a Yankees cap on the Yankee legend's head. It looked right and it also enabled Berra to shield the sun while he sat between Torre and Coach Don Zimmer during an intrasquad game. The Yankees were on the field and so was Berra. Perfect.

"I haven't worn a baseball cap in a long time," Berra said.

While Berra did not admit it, he probably has not worn a Yankee cap since George Steinbrenner unceremoniously dismissed him 16 games into the 1985 season. Since Steinbrenner apologized to Berra for the atrocious way he had treated him and ended almost 14 years of friction in a meeting on Jan. 5, Berra feels comfortable being a Yankee again.

"I thought he was getting cheated by this whole thing," Torre said. "There's a lot of things he enjoys that he didn't get the chance to do."

Now Berra is doing them. Torre said Steinbrenner wanted to have Berra throw out the first pitch at Yankee Stadium with Joe DiMaggio, if he is healthy, and the 73-year-old Berra said he would oblige if he was asked. Berra would not confirm that he would attend Old-Timers' Day, but it is likely Steinbrenner and Torre can convince him.

"We'll see what happens," said Berra, who also sat in Steinbrenner's private box.

Even though Berra was happy to be back, he was candid when someone asked him if he always knew he would make amends with Steinbrenner.

"I don't know," Berra said. "He called. He called and apologized. He said the right things. If he didn't, I wouldn't be here today."

Yogi Joins Some Famous Foes from Brooklyn

By Dave Anderson • May 23, 1999

LITTLE FALLS, N.J.—Up on the screen in grainy black-and-white film, the Yankees were playing the Dodgers in their six World Series from 1947 to 1956 and every so often Yogi Berra would appear, swinging a bat or in his catcher's mask. And now, in the Yogi Berra Museum's theater, Lawrence Peter Berra himself stood up Friday for his induction into, of all things, the Brooklyn Dodger Hall of Fame.

"They weren't easy," he was saying, alluding to those Dodger teams. "They were a real good ball club."

Behind him, Joe Pignatano, a former Mets coach and once a Dodger catcher, interrupted, saying with a smile, "You still know how to lie." Yogi never blinked.

Yogi Berra at home in Yankee blue. (Barton Silverman/The New York Times)

"They had a real good ball club," Yogi said firmly. "We just beat 'em, that's all."

Beat 'em in five of those six World Series, and more often than not, Yogi Berra was in the middle of what was going on. He caught Don Larsen's perfect game in 1956 and over those six Series, he hit eight homers and knocked in 21 runs with a .298 average, including 3 homers and 10 runs batted in in 1956, the last Series in Ebbets Field.

Along with dozens of familiar Brooklyn Dodgers, this Yankee folk hero is now in perhaps the only pantheon to also honor famous foes. Bobby Thomson is in it. So are Stan Musial, Ralph Kiner, Johnny Vander Meer, Warren Spahn, Johnny Sain, Robin Roberts, Curt Simmons, and two other Yankees—Tommy Henrich and Johnny Kucks.

Not everybody remembers Johnny Kucks, but anybody who was in Brooklyn in 1956 remembers.

Kucks, a sinkerball right-hander with an 18–9 record who had worked twice in relief in that Series, pitched a 9–0 six-hitter supported by Berra's pair of two-run homers off Don Newcombe, the Dodger ace with a 27–7 record that season. Berra also hit a grand slam off Newcombe in the second game.

"On those two homers in the seventh game, Newk threw two good pitches—one away, one in," Berra recalled. "I just saw the ball good. Before one of 'em, Roy Campanella didn't hold a foul tip that would have been a third strike."

In 1955, when the Dodgers won their only World Series representing Brooklyn, Jackie Robinson stole home in the opener at Yankee Stadium with Whitey Ford pitching and Frank Kellert at bat. When Bill Summers, an American League umpire, ruled Robinson safe, Berra hopped around in protest.

"He was out," Berra was saying now.

"Out by how much?" a listener asked.

"He was out," Berra repeated. "Out."

In the sixth inning of that Series' seventh game, with the Dodgers leading, 2-0, Billy Martin on second and Gil McDougald on first, the left-hander Johnny Podres threw a high outside pitch. Berra swung and lifted

Yogi Berra and Don Larsen discuss their time together on the diamond. (Michelle V. Agins/The New York Times)

a short fly ball down the left-field line. "If Amoros wasn't there, it's a hit," Berra said. "Amoros was fast. He ran a long ways." Sandy Amoros was also left-handed. He stuck out his glove, caught the ball on the run, then threw to shortstop Pee Wee Reese, who threw to first baseman Gil Hodges to double up McDougald.

"Most people don't know," Yogi said, "that the Dodgers wanted to sign me."

Growing up in St. Louis as an outfielder and third baseman, Berra was scouted by the Cardinals, but their general manager, Branch Rickey, played down Berra's potential. "Rickey told me I'd never be a big league ball-player," Berra recalled.

Rickey, however, was about to desert the Cardinals to become the Dodgers' president. He was hoping to sign Berra as a Dodger farmhand. But in 1943 the Yankees signed Berra.

"After I signed with the Yankees," Berra said, "I got a telegram from Rickey to join the Dodgers in spring training." By the 1947 Series, Berra was the Yankees' rookie catcher at Ebbets Field as the right-hander Floyd (Bill) Bevens, leading, 2–1, went into the ninth inning of the fourth game with a no-hitter. With two out, Al Gionfriddo, running for Carl Furillo, tried to steal second.

"I threw high," Berra remembered. "With a good throw, maybe Bevens gets his no-hitter, but I was a terrible catcher then."

Gionfriddo was safe. Pete Reiser walked; Eddie Miksis ran for him. Harry (Cookie) Lavagetto broke up the no-hitter with a double off the right-field wall as Gionfriddo and Miksis scored. The Dodgers won, 3–2, but the Yankees won that Series in seven games.

But what if the Dodgers had signed Lawrence Peter Berra?

Maybe the Dodgers instead of the Yankees would have won five of those six World Series from 1947 to 1956. And when Roy Campanella arrived in 1948 as the Dodgers' catcher, who would have been moved to another position, probably left field?

"Me," Yogi Berra said. "I was a terrible catcher then." ■

Yogi Berra sits in the dugout with Ron Guidry during Spring Training. (Barton Silverman/The New York Times)

Cone Pitches Perfect Game on Yogi Berra Day

By Murray Chass • July 19, 1999

In an improbable setting, David Cone performed an improbable feat yesterday. He pitched the Yankees' second perfect game in little more than a year, and he did it playing in front of Don Larsen, who pitched a perfect World Series game for the Yankees in 1956.

Larsen was at Yankee Stadium to help celebrate Yogi Berra Day, and after Larsen threw the ceremonial first pitch to Berra, Cone took command of the mound and retired all 27 Montreal batters he faced as the Yankees clubbed the Expos, 6–0. It was only the 16th perfect game in major league history.

Following David Wells's perfect game against Minnesota by one year, two months and one day, Cone made the Yankees the first team to pitch perfect games in successive seasons and the first to have three perfect games to their credit.

"I probably have a better chance of winning the lottery than this happening today," an exuberant Cone said. "What an honor. All the Yankee legends here. Don Larsen in the park. Yogi Berra Day. It makes you stop and think about the Yankee magic and the mystique of this ball park." ■

Yankee teammates pile on David Cone after he pitched a perfect game on July 18, 1999 (Barton Silverman/The New York Times)

Berra, 80, a Folk Hero and a Philosopher, Has Observed a Lot by Watching

By Dave Anderson • May 12, 2005

On the stucco building at the far end of the Montclair State campus, Yogi Berra's large signature precedes the words "Museum and Learning Center." Seldom have any words fit anyone's name so well. As a folk hero and philosopher, Yogi Berra is a living, walking museum. And whenever you're around him, you learn something, either about him or about the world. Such as his reaction to turning 80 today.

"I don't want to know how old I am," he said in his grunting voice. "I want to go backwards."

Go backward to being 79 next year, then 78, then 77. Go backward, ideally, to when he was a Hall of Fame catcher and outfielder on 10 Yankees teams that won the World Series in the '40s, '50s and '60s. If only this season's Yankees had a young Yogi in their lineup, they wouldn't be struggling to get to .500, but he still had faith in them.

"Nothing's over," he said with a quick smile, "until it's over."

And to people everywhere, nothing's as familiar as Yogi's face.

"I got a face they can't forget," he said last week, sitting in his office at the little baseball museum visited by 20,000 children each year. "Wherever I go, people say, 'You're not Yogi Berra, are you?' and I'll say, 'No, I just look like him.'"

He doesn't fool them. They know he must be Yogi Berra because nobody else looks like him. Or talks like him.

"They ask for a Yogi-ism," he said, "but I say, 'I didn't even know 'em when I said 'em.' They just come out."

Yogi is now the pinstriped symbol of the Yankees' winning tradition. He throws out the first pitch on opening day, as he did yesterday, when he and his museum were honored at Yankee Stadium, with the Yankees donating $25,000 to the museum.

Yogi was born in 1925, and his life has spanned all but one of the Yankees' 26 World Series triumphs. Officially a Yankees senior adviser, he often visits Joe Torre in the manager's office, chats with the coaches and players, then goes upstairs to watch the game, sometimes with George Steinbrenner.

"If he's in, he makes me sit in his office with him and watch it on TV," he said. "He's very superstitious. If they don't score, he wanders. Then I go out and sit in his box."

During the early workouts at Spring Training, Yogi, who once said, "You can observe a lot by watching," roams the Yankees' complex in Tampa, Florida, mostly observing the younger players, particularly in the exhibition games.

"In practice, they do everything good," he said. "I like to see what they do in the games."

Yogi also observes the Yankees on television at his home in nearby Montclair—the home that once prompted his driving directions to a visitor, "When you come to a fork in the road, take it." And he watches those games as if he were still in the batter's box.

"You second-guess yourself," he said. "You say to yourself, 'What did you take that pitch for?'"

As a slugger with 358 home runs and 1,430 runs batted in, Yogi was a bad-ball hitter who seldom took a pitch. His motto: If he could see it, he could hit it.

"But during the Yankee commercials, I turn to the Mets," he said. "I was there 10 years, you know. I hope Willie Randolph does good."

When the Yankees fired him as manager after the 1964 World Series loss to the Cardinals, he joined the Mets as a coach and later succeeded Gil Hodges as manager. He guided the Mets to the 1973 pennant, but the Oakland Athletics won that World Series.

"Those are my two regrets," he said. "Getting to the seventh game of those two World Series and we didn't win both times."

But he had more good times than bad. He wears his Hall of Fame ring on the ring finger of his left hand,

Yogi Berra is introduced at the 65th annual Old Timers Day at the Stadium. (Barton Silverman/The New York Times)

his 1953 World Series ring on the little finger of his right hand.

"When we won in '53, that was our fifth World Series in a row," he said. "Nobody else did that."

Yogi has 10 World Series rings, many of them a gift from Steinbrenner to commemorate their 1999 truce after Yogi's refusal to go to Yankee Stadium after he was fired in 1985 as manager after a 6–10 start. But for some of Yogi's early Series victories, the Yankees didn't always get rings.

"They asked us what we wanted then," he said. "One year we got a silver cigarette box with everybody's autograph on it. Another year we got a silver tray with the autographs. They're nice."

And when asked how he will celebrate his 80th birthday, Yogi Berra talked about "having a little barbecue" today in his backyard with his wife, Carmen, and "the kids and the grandkids"—sons Larry, Timmy, and Dale, along with their wives and their 10 sons and daughters.

"I'm just thankful for living this long," he said. "And maybe a few more years."

Preferably backward. ∎

First Pitch at Yankee Stadium? Yogi, of Course

By Tyler Kepner • April 15, 2009

If the Yankees had picked anybody else to throw out the ceremonial first pitch at their new stadium Thursday, it just wouldn't have seemed right. Yogi Berra, 83 years young, will do the honors before the Yankees host Cleveland at 1:05 PM.

The home plate and pitching rubber to be used Thursday are the same set that closed out the old Yankee Stadium in September. When the game is over, the plate and the rubber will be moved to the Yankees Museum, located in the ballpark. ∎

65th annual Old Timers Day at the Stadium. Whitey Ford, Mickey Rivers, and Yogi Berra. (Barton Silverman/The New York Times)

It Happens Every Spring: "Driving Mr. Yogi"

By Harvey Araton • February 24, 2011

TAMPA, Fla.—With all the yearly changes made by the Yankees, Yogi Berra's arrival at their spring training base adds a timeless quality to baseball's most historic franchise.

Berra, the catching legend and pop culture icon, slips back into the uniform with the famous and familiar No. 8. He checks into the same hotel in the vicinity of George M. Steinbrenner Field and requests the same room. He plans his days methodically—wake up at 6 AM, breakfast at 6:30, depart for the complex by 7—and steps outside to be greeted by the same driver he has had for the past dozen years.

The driver has a rather famous name, and nickname, as well.

"It's like I'm the valet," said Ron Guidry, the former star pitcher known around the Yankees as Gator for his Louisiana roots. "Actually, I am the valet."

When Berra arrived on Tuesday afternoon from New Jersey for his three- to four-week stay, Guidry, as always, was waiting for him at Tampa International Airport. Since Berra forgave George Steinbrenner in 1999 for firing him as the manager in 1985 through a subordinate and ended a 14-year boycott of the team, Guidry has been his faithful friend and loyal shepherd.

Guidry had a custom-made cap to certify his proud standing. The inscription reads, "Driving Mr. Yogi."

"He's a good guy," Berra, the Yankees' 85-year-old honorary patriarch, said during an interview at his museum in Little Falls, New Jersey. "We hang out together in spring training."

By "hanging out," Berra means being in uniform with the Yankees by day and having dinner with Guidry by night. That is, until Guidry, who loves to cook and rents a two-bedroom apartment across the road from where Berra stays, demands a break from their spring training rotation of the five restaurants that meet Berra's approval.

"See, I really love the old man, but because of what we share—which is something very special—I can treat him more as a friend and I can say, 'Get your butt in my truck or you're staying,'" Guidry said. "He likes that kind of camaraderie, wants to be treated like everybody else, but because of who he is, that's not how everybody around here treats him.

"So I'll say, 'Yogi, tonight we're going to Fleming's, then to Lee Roy Selmon's tomorrow, and then the night after that you stay in your damn room, have a ham sandwich or whatever, because the world doesn't revolve around you and I'm taking a night off.'"

Berra played 18 years for the Yankees, from 1946 to 1963, and was part of 10 World Series champions. Guidry pitched from the mid-1970s through 1988, played on two World Series winners and was a Cy Young Award winner in 1978, when he was 25–3 with a 1.74 earned run average.

While Guidry was blossoming into one of baseball's premier left-handers, Berra was a coach on Manager Billy Martin's staff (and later became Guidry's manager). They dressed at adjacent stalls in the clubhouse of the old Yankee Stadium. Eager to learn, Guidry would pepper Berra with questions about what he, as a former catcher, thought of hitters.

Berra would say, "You got a great catcher right over there," nodding in the direction of Thurman Munson. But Guidry persisted, and their bond was formed.

In offering his companionship, Guidry discovered that he was the luckier side of the partnership spanning generations of Yankees greatness.

"I never got to pitch against Ted Williams, for example," Guidry said. "I'd say, 'Yogi, when you guys had to go to Boston and you had to face Williams, how did you work him?' You know, he's like an encyclopedia, and that's what I loved, all the stories and just being with him. If he's not the most beloved man in America, I don't know who is."

Ron Guidry picking up Yogi Berra at the Tampa airport on Feb. 24, 2011, (Eric Linsmeir/The New York Times)

He has asked Berra to stay with him in his apartment, but Berra prefers the hotel. "I mean, the only time we're really not together is when he's asleep," Guidry said. "But you can't get him out of there because that's how it's been. You can't change him. When he does it one day, it's going to be that way for the next 1,000 days."

That is why Guidry considers his supreme achievement in their dozen years as the Yankees' odd couple to be the day—he guessed it was five years ago—that he persuaded Berra to try a Cajun culinary staple.

Every spring, Guidry brings from his home near Lafayette, Louisiana, about 200 frog legs and a flour mix to fry them. One day, he took a batch to the clubhouse to share with the former pitching coach Mel Stottlemyre, turned to Berra and said, "Try these." Berra shook his head, as if Guidry were offering him tofu.

Guidry told him, "You don't try it, we're not going out to supper tonight."

Berra relented, and soon a dinner of frog legs, green beans wrapped in bacon and a sweet potato at Guidry's apartment—usually timed to a weekend of NCAA basketball tournament games—became as much a rite of spring as pitchers and catchers.

"He calls me at home this year to remind me about the frogs' legs — 'Did you get 'em yet?" Guidry said. "I said, 'Yogi, it's freaking January, calm down.'"

Since taking a fall outside his home last summer that required hospitalization and a period of inactivity, Berra has slowed. His voice is softer. His words seem to be sparser.

"I know Carmen feels he's going to be fine and occupied because I'm around," Guidry said. "But this year may be harder than the rest because of what happened. I'm just going to have to watch a little more closely to see what he can do."

The first item on Berra's agenda, he said, would be to go shopping.

"He buys his roast beef, I buy my bottle of vodka," Berra said, with a twinkle in his eye. "We get along real good." ∎

Derek Jeter acknowledges Yogi Berra after receiving his World Series ring on April 13, 2010. (AP Images)

Yogi Berra, Hall of Fame Catcher for the Yankees, Dies at 90

By Bruce Weber • September 23, 2015

Yogi Berra, one of baseball's greatest catchers and characters, who as a player was a mainstay of 10 Yankee championship teams and as a manager led both the Yankees and Mets to the World Series—but who may be more widely known as an ungainly but lovable cultural figure, inspiring a cartoon character and issuing a seemingly limitless supply of unwittingly witty epigrams known as Yogi-isms—died on Tuesday. He was 90.

His death was reported by the Yankees and by the Yogi Berra Museum and Learning Center in Little Falls, N.J. Before moving to an assisted living facility in nearby West Caldwell, in 2012, Berra had lived for many years in neighboring Montclair.

In 1949, early in Berra's Yankee career, his manager assessed him this way in an interview in The Sporting News: "Mr. Berra," Casey Stengel said, "is a very strange fellow of very remarkable abilities."

And so he was, and so he proved to be. Universally known simply as Yogi, probably the second most recognizable nickname in sports—even Yogi was not the Babe—Berra was not exactly an unlikely hero, but he was often portrayed as one: an All-Star for 15 consecutive seasons whose skills were routinely underestimated; a well-built, appealingly open-faced man whose physical appearance was often belittled; and a prolific winner—not to mention a successful leader—whose intellect was a target of humor if not outright derision.

That he triumphed on the diamond again and again in spite of his perceived shortcomings was certainly a source of his popularity. So was the delight with which his famous, if not always documentable, pronouncements, somehow both nonsensical and sagacious, were received.

"You can observe a lot just by watching," he is reputed to have declared once, describing his strategy as a manager.

"If you can't imitate him," he advised a young player who was mimicking the batting stance of the great slugger Frank Robinson, "don't copy him."

"When you come to a fork in the road, take it," he said, giving directions to his house. Either path, it turned out, got you there.

"Nobody goes there anymore," he said of a popular restaurant. "It's too crowded."

Whether Berra actually uttered the many things attributed to him, or was the first to say them, or phrased them precisely the way they were reported, has long been a matter of speculation. Berra himself published a book in 1998 called "The Yogi Book: I

Really Didn't Say Everything I Said!" But the Yogi-isms testified to a character—goofy and philosophical, flighty and down to earth—that came to define the man.

Berra's Yogi-ness was exploited in advertisements for myriad products, among them Puss 'n Boots cat food and Miller Lite beer, but perhaps most famously, Yoo-Hoo chocolate drink. Asked if Yoo-Hoo was hyphenated, he is said to have replied, "No, ma'am, it isn't even carbonated."

If not exactly a Yogi-ism, it was the kind of response that might have come from Berra's ursine namesake, the affable animated character Yogi Bear, who made his debut in 1958.

The character Yogi Berra may even have overshadowed the Hall of Fame ballplayer Yogi Berra, obscuring what a remarkable athlete he was. A notorious "bad ball" hitter—he swung at a lot of pitches that were not strikes but mashed them anyway—he was fearsome in the clutch and the most durable and consistently productive Yankee during the period of the team's most relentless success.

In addition, as a catcher he played the most physically grueling and concentration-demanding position on the field. (For a respite from the chores and challenges of crouching behind the plate, Berra, who played before the designated hitter rule took effect in the American League in 1973, occasionally played the outfield.)

Stengel, the Hall of Fame manager whose shrewdness and talent were also often underestimated, recognized Berra's gifts. He referred to Berra, even as a young player, as his assistant manager and compared him favorably to star catchers of previous eras like Mickey Cochrane, Gabby Hartnett, and Bill Dickey. "You could look it up" was Stengel's catchphrase, and indeed the record book declares that Berra was among the greatest catchers in the history of the game, some say the greatest of all.

Berra's career batting average of .285 was not as high as that of his Yankee predecessor Dickey (.313), but Berra hit more home runs (358) and drove in more runs (1,430). Widely praised by pitchers for his astute pitch-calling, Berra led the American League in assists five times, and from 1957 through 1959 went 148

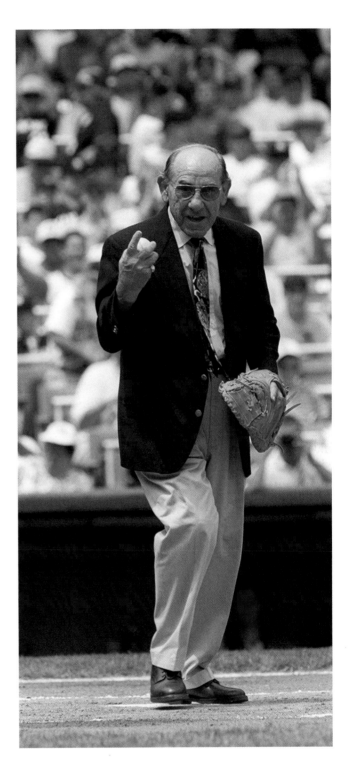

Yogi Berra preparing to throw out the first pitch on Yogi Day, July 18, 1999. (Barton Silverman/The New York Times)

consecutive games behind the plate without making an error, a major league record at the time—though he was not a defensive wizard from the start.

Dickey, Berra explained, "learned me all his experience."

On defense, he certainly surpassed Mike Piazza, the best-hitting catcher of recent vintage—and maybe ever. Johnny Bench, whose Cincinnati Reds teams of the 1970s were known as the Big Red Machine, and Berra were comparable in offensive production, except that Bench struck out three times as often. Berra whiffed a mere 414 times in more than 8,300 plate appearances over 19 seasons—an astonishingly small ratio for a power hitter.

Others—Carlton Fisk, Gary Carter, and Ivan Rodriguez among them—also deserve consideration in a discussion of great catchers, but none was clearly superior to Berra on offense or defense. Only Roy Campanella, a contemporary rival who played for the Brooklyn Dodgers and faced Berra in the World Series six times before his career was ended by an auto accident, equaled Berra's total of three Most Valuable Player awards. And though Berra did not win the award in 1950—his teammate Phil Rizzuto did—he gave one of the greatest season-long performances by a catcher that year, hitting .322, smacking 28 homers, and driving in 124 runs.

Berra's career was punctuated by storied episodes. In Game 3 of the 1947 World Series against the Dodgers, he hit the first pinch-hit home run in Series history, and in Game 4 he was behind the plate for what was almost the first no-hitter and was instead a stunning loss. With two out in the ninth inning and two men on base with walks, the Yankees' starter, Bill Bevens, gave up a double to Cookie Lavagetto that cleared the bases and won the game.

In September 1951, once again on the brink of a no-hitter, this one by Allie Reynolds against the Red Sox, Berra made one of baseball's legendary errors. With two out in the ninth inning, Ted Williams hit a towering foul ball between home plate and the Yankee dugout; it looked like the end of the game, sealing Reynolds's second no-hitter of the season and making him the first American League pitcher to accomplish that feat. But as the ball plummeted, it was caught in a gust of wind; Berra lunged backward, and it deflected off his glove as he went sprawling.

Amazingly, on the next pitch, Williams hit an almost identical pop-up, and this time Berra caught it.

In the first game of the 1955 World Series against Brooklyn, the Yankees were ahead, 6-4, in the top of the eighth when the Dodgers' Jackie Robinson stole home. The plate umpire Bill Summers called him safe, and Berra went berserk, gesticulating in Summers's face and creating one of the enduring images of an on-the-field tantrum. The Yankees won the game, though not the Series—it was the only time Brooklyn got the better of Berra's Yanks—but Berra never forgot the moment. More than 50 years later, he signed a photograph of the play for President Obama, writing, "Dear Mr. President, He was out!"

During the 1956 Series, again against Brooklyn, Berra was at the center of another indelible image, this one of sheer joy, when he leapt into the arms of Don Larsen, who had just struck out Dale Mitchell to end Game 5 and complete the only perfect game (and only no-hitter) in World Series history.

When reporters gathered at Berra's locker after the game, he greeted them mischievously. "So," he said, "what's new?"

Beyond the historic moments and individual accomplishments, what most distinguished Berra's career was how often he won. From 1946 to 1985, as a player, coach, and manager, Berra appeared in a remarkable 21 World Series. Playing on powerful Yankee teams with teammates like Rizzuto and Joe DiMaggio early on and then Whitey Ford and Mickey Mantle, Berra starred on World Series winners in 1947, '49, '50, '51, '52, '53, '56, and '58. He was a backup player on the championship teams of 1961 and '62. (He also played on World Series losers in 1955, '57, '60, and '63.) All told, his Yankee teams won the American League pennant 14 out of 17 years. He still holds Series records for games played, plate appearances, hits, and doubles.

Roger Maris, Yogi Berra, and Mickey Mantle pose together before a game against the Red Sox at Fenway Park on July 22, 1961. (AP Images)

No other player has been a champion so often.

Lawrence Peter Berra was born on May 12, 1925, in the Italian enclave of St. Louis known as the Hill, which also fostered the baseball career of his boyhood friend Joe Garagiola. Berra was the fourth of five children. His father, Pietro, a construction worker and a bricklayer, and his mother, Paulina, were immigrants from Malvaglio, a northern Italian village near Milan. (As an adult, on a visit to his ancestral home, Berra took in a performance of "Tosca" at La Scala. "It was pretty good," he said. "Even the music was nice.")

As a boy, Berra was known as Larry, or Lawdie, as his mother pronounced it. As recounted in "Yogi Ber-ra: Eternal Yankee," a 2009 biography by Allen Bar-ra, one day in his early teens, young Larry and some friends had gone to the movies and were watching a travelogue about India when a Hindu yogi appeared on the screen sitting cross-legged. His posture struck one of the friends as precisely the way Berra sat on the ground as he waited his turn at bat. From that day on, he was Yogi Berra.

An ardent athlete but an indifferent student, Berra dropped out of school after the eighth grade. He played American Legion ball and worked odd jobs. As teenagers, both he and Garagiola tried out with the St. Louis Cardinals and were offered contracts by the

Phil Linz douses Yogi Berra with champagne after the Yankees clinch the 1964 pennant. (Ernie Sisto/ The New York Times)

Cardinals' general manager, Branch Rickey. But Garagiola's came with a $500 signing bonus and Berra's just $250, so Berra declined to sign. (This was a harbinger of deals to come. Berra, whose salary as a player reached $65,000 in 1961, substantial for that era, would prove to be a canny contract negotiator, almost always extracting concessions from the Yankees' penurious general manager George Weiss.)

In the meantime, the St. Louis Browns—they later moved to Baltimore and became the Orioles—also wanted to sign Berra but were not willing to pay any bonus at all. Then, the day after the 1942 World Series, in which the Cardinals beat the Yankees, a Yankee coach showed up at Berra's parents' house and offered him a minor-league contract—along with the elusive $500.

Berra's professional baseball life began in Virginia in 1943 with the Norfolk Tars of the Class B Piedmont League. In 111 games he hit .253 and led the league's catchers in errors, but he once had 12 hits and drove in 23 runs over two consecutive games. It was a promising start, but World War II put his career on hold. Berra joined the Navy. He took part in the invasion of Normandy and, two months later, in Operation Dragoon, an Allied assault on Marseilles in which he was bloodied by a bullet and earned a Purple Heart.

In 1946, after his discharge, he was assigned to the Newark Bears, then the Yankees' top farm team. He played outfield and catcher and hit .314 with 15 home runs and 59 runs batted in 77 games, though his fielding still lacked polish; in one instance he hit an umpire with a throw from behind the plate meant for second base. Nonetheless, the Yankees summoned him in September. In his first big league game he had two hits, including a home run.

As a Yankee, Berra became a fan favorite, partly because of his superior play—he batted .305 and drove in 98 runs in 1948, his second full season—and partly because of his humility and guilelessness. In 1947, honored at Sportsman's Park in St. Louis, a nervous Berra told the hometown crowd, "I want to thank everyone for making this night necessary."

Berra was a hit with sportswriters, too, though they often portrayed him as a baseball idiot savant, an apelike, barely literate devotee of comic books and movies who spoke fractured English. So was born the Yogi caricature, of the triumphant rube.

"Even today," Life magazine wrote in July 1949, "he has only pity for people who clutter their brains with such unnecessary and frivolous matters as literature and the sciences, not to mention grammar and orthography."

Collier's magazine declared, "With a body that only an anthropologist could love, the 185-pound Berra could pass easily as a member of the Neanderthal A.C."

Berra tended to take the gibes in stride. If he was ugly, he was said to have remarked, it did not matter at the plate. "I never saw nobody hit one with his face," he was quoted as saying. But when writers chided him about his girlfriend, Carmen Short, saying he was too unattractive to marry her, he responded, according to Colliers, "I'm human, ain't I?"

Berra outlasted the ridicule. He married Ms. Short in 1949, and the marriage endured until her death in 2014. He is survived by their three sons—Tim, who played professional football for the Baltimore Colts; Dale, a former infielder for the Yankees, Pirates and Astros; and Lawrence Jr.—as well as 11 grandchildren and a great-grandson.

Certainly, assessments of Berra changed over the years.

"He has continued to allow people to regard him as an amiable clown because it brings him quick acceptance, despite ample proof, onfield and off, that he is intelligent, shrewd and opportunistic," Robert Lipsyte wrote in *The New York Times* in October 1963.

At the time, Berra had just concluded his career as a Yankee player and the team had named him manager, a role in which he would continue to find success, though not with the same regularity he enjoyed as a player and not without drama and disappointment. Indeed things began badly. The Yankees, an aging team in 1964, played listless ball through much of the summer, and in mid-August they lost four straight games in Chicago to the first-place White Sox, leading to one of the kookier episodes of Berra's career.

On the team bus to O'Hare Airport, the reserve infielder Phil Linz began playing "Mary Had a Little Lamb" on the harmonica. Berra, in a foul mood over the losing streak, told him to knock it off, but Linz did not. (In another version of the story, Linz asked Mickey Mantle what Berra had said, and Mantle responded, "He said, 'Play it louder.' ") Suddenly the harmonica went flying, having been either knocked out of Linz's hands by Berra or thrown at Berra by Linz. (Players on the bus had different recollections.)

News reports of the incident made it sound as if Berra had lost control of the team, and though the Yankees caught and passed the White Sox in September, winning the pennant, Ralph Houk, the general manager, fired Berra after the team lost a seven-game World Series to St. Louis, in a bizarre move replacing him with the Cardinals' manager, Johnny Keane.

Keane's Yankees finished sixth in 1965.

Berra, meanwhile, moved across town, taking a job as a coach for the famously awful Mets under Stengel, who was finishing his career in Flushing. The team continued its mythic floundering until 1969, when the so-called Miracle Mets, with Gil Hodges as manager—and Berra coaching first base—won the World Series.

After Hodges died before the start of the 1972 season, Berra replaced him. He was inducted into the Hall of Fame in that summer, but the Mets team he inherited faltered, finishing third, and for most of the 1973 season they were worse. In mid-August, the team was well under .500 and in sixth place, when Berra uttered perhaps the most famous Yogi-ism of all.

"It ain't over till it's over," he said (or words to that effect), and, lo and behold, the Mets got hot, squeaking by the Cardinals to win the National League's Eastern Division title.

They then beat the Reds in the League Championship Series before losing to the Oakland Athletics in the World Series. Berra was rewarded for the resurgence with a three-year contract, but the Mets were dreadful in 1974, finishing fifth, and the next year, on Aug. 6, with the team in third place and having lost five straight games, Berra was fired.

Once again he switched leagues and city boroughs, returning to the Bronx as a Yankee coach, and in 1984

the owner, George M. Steinbrenner, named him to replace the volatile Billy Martin as manager. The team finished third that year, but during spring training in 1985, Steinbrenner promised him that he would finish the season as Yankee manager no matter what. However, after just 16 games (the Yankees were 6-10) the impatient and imperious Steinbrenner fired Berra anyway, bringing back Martin—and worse than breaking his word, perhaps, sending an underling to deliver the bad news.

The firing, which had an added sting because Berra's son Dale had recently joined the Yankees, provoked one of baseball's legendary feuds, and for 14 years Berra refused to set foot in Yankee Stadium, a period during which he coached four seasons for the Houston Astros.

In the meantime private donors helped establish the Yogi Berra Museum and Learning Center on the New Jersey campus of Montclair State University, which awarded Berra an honorary doctorate of humanities in 1996 and where a minor league ballpark, Yogi Berra Stadium, opened in 1998. A tribute to Berra with exhibits on his career, the museum runs programs for children dealing with baseball history. In January 1999, Steinbrenner, who died in 2010, went there to make amends.

"I know I made a mistake by not letting you go personally," he told Berra. "It's the worst mistake I ever made in baseball."

Berra chose not to quibble with the semi-apology. To welcome him back into the Yankee fold, the team held a Yogi Berra Day on July 18, 1999. Also invited was Don Larsen, who threw out the ceremonial first pitch, which Berra caught.

Incredibly, in the game that day, David Cone of the Yankees pitched a perfect game.

It was, as Berra may or may not have said in another context, "déjà vu all over again," a fittingly climactic episode for a wondrous baseball life. ■

Yogi Berra in one of so many springs spent in pinstripes. (Richard Perry/The New York Times)